THE
MICHELIN
GUIDE

WASHINGTON DC

2018

THE MICHELIN GUIDE'S COMMITMENTS

Whether they are in Japan, the USA, China or Europe, our inspectors apply the same criteria to judge the quality of each and every establishment that they visit. The MICHELIN guide commands a **worldwide reputation** thanks to the commitments we make to our readers—and we reiterate these below:

Our inspectors make **anonymous visits** to restaurants to gauge the quality of cuisine offered to the everyday customer. They pay their own bill and make no indication of their presence. These visits are supplemented by comprehensive monitoring of information—our readers' comments are one valuable source, and are always taken into consideration.

Our choice of establishments is a completely **independent** one, made for the benefit of our readers alone. Decisions are discussed by the inspectors and editor, with the most important considered at the global level. Inclusion in the Guide is always free of charge.

The Guide offers a **selection** of the best restaurants in each category of comfort and price. A recommendation in the Guide is an honor in itself, and defines the establishment among the "best of the best."

All practical information, the classifications, and awards are revised and updated every year to ensure the most **reliable information** possible.

The standards and criteria for the classifications are the same in all countries covered by the MICHELIN guides. Our system is used worldwide and easy to apply when selecting a restaurant.

As part of Michelin's ongoing commitment to improving **travel and mobility**, we do everything possible to make vacations and eating out a pleasure.

THE MICHELIN GUIDE'S SYMBOLS

AVERAGE PRICES

⊘	Under $25
$$	$25 to $50
$$$	$50 to $75
$$$$	Over $75

FACILITIES & SERVICES

⬙	Notable wine list
🍸	Notable cocktail list
🍺	Notable beer list
🍶	Notable sake list
♿	Wheelchair accessible
⛱	Outdoor dining
⊡	Private dining room
🍳	Breakfast
◔	Brunch
✦	Dim sum
🚗	Valet parking
💵	Cash only

RESTAURANT CLASSIFICATIONS BY COMFORT
More pleasant if in red

⧻	Small plates
✗	Comfortable
✗✗	Quite comfortable
✗✗✗	Very comfortable
✗✗✗✗	Top class comfortable
✗✗✗✗✗	Luxury in the traditional style

THE MICHELIN DISTINCTIONS FOR GOOD CUISINE

STARS

Our famous one ✿, two ✿✿ and three ✿✿✿ stars
identify establishments serving the highest quality
cuisine – taking into account the quality of ingredients,
the mastery of techniques and flavors, the levels of
creativity and, of course, consistency.

✿✿✿   Exceptional cuisine, worth a special journey

✿✿   Excellent cuisine, worth a detour

✿   High quality cooking, worth a stop

BIB GOURMAND

Inspectors' favorites for good value.

MICHELIN PLATE

Good cooking.
Fresh ingredients, carefully
prepared: simply a good meal.

DEAR READER,

It's been an exciting year for the entire team at the MICHELIN guides in North America, and it is with great pride that we present you with our 2018 edition to Washington DC. Over the past year our inspectors have extended their reach to include a variety of establishments and multiplied their anonymous visits to restaurants in our selection in order to accurately reflect the rich culinary diversity this great city has to offer.

As part of the Guide's highly confidential and meticulous evaluation process, our inspectors have methodically eaten their way through the entire city with a mission to marshal the finest in each category for your enjoyment. While they are expertly trained professionals in the food industry, the Guides remain consumer-driven and provide comprehensive choices to accommodate your every comfort, taste, and budget. By dining and drinking as "everyday" customers, they are able to experience and evaluate the same level of service and cuisine as any other guest. This past year has seen some unique advancements in DC's dining scene.

Our company's founders, Édouard and André Michelin, published the first MICHELIN guide in 1900, to provide motorists with useful information about where they could service and repair their cars as well as find a good quality meal. In 1926, the star-rating system was introduced, whereby outstanding establishments are awarded for excellence in cuisine. Over the decades we have made many new enhancements to the Guide, and the local team here in Washington DC eagerly carries on these traditions.

As we take consumer feedback seriously, please feel free to contact us at: michelin.guides@michelin.com. You may also follow our Inspectors on Instagram (@michelininspectors) as they chow their way around town. We thank you for your patronage and truly hope that the MICHELIN guide will remain your preferred reference to Washington DC's restaurants.

CONTENTS

COMMITMENTS   3
THE MICHELIN GUIDE'S SYMBOLS   4
DEAR READER   7

▪ RESTAURANTS   10

▪ MAPS   80

DUPONT CIRCLE, LOGAN CIRCLE
& FOGGY BOTTOM ·······82
COLUMBIA HEIGHTS, U STREET
& ADAMS MORGAN ·······84
PENN QUARTER & CHINATOWN·······86
CAPITOL HILL & NAVY YARD ·······87
FOXHALL·······88
CLEVELAND PARK ·······88
GEORGETOWN·······88
FLORIDA AVE & GALLAUDET UNIVERSITY····89

▪ INDEXES

ALPHABETICAL LIST OF RESTAURANTS   92
RESTAURANTS BY CUISINE   96
STARRED RESTAURANTS   100
BIB GOURMAND   101
UNDER $25   102

WASHINGTON DC

ACADIANA 🍴

Southern

XX | 🍴 💠 🚬 🛋

With its classic take on N'awlins fare (think fried green tomatoes, turtle soup, and charbroiled oysters) Acadiana spices things up—way up—in a neighborhood best known for its convention center and business-minded clientele. Begin with a fluffy biscuit topped with sweet-hot red pepper jelly before tucking into one of the Creole or Cajun classics like jambalaya or smoked chicken and andouille sausage gumbo. The kitchen's take on shrimp and grits, dolled up with strips of tender Tasso ham and a crispy-gooey cheddar cheese-grit cake, takes the Southern staple to bold new levels.

And though we wouldn't dare tell mama, the buttery pecan pie, topped with vanilla ice cream and layered with roasted pecans and caramel, is every bit as good as hers.

◼ 901 New York Ave. NW (at 9th St.)
🚇 Mt Vernon Sq
☏ (202) 408-8848 — **WEB:** www.acadianarestaurant.com
◼ Lunch Sun – Fri   Dinner nightly   **PRICE: $$**

AL TIRAMISU 🍴

Italian

X

With two decades under its belt, it's clear that Al Tiramisu is no flash in the pan. The unassuming restaurant is classic Italian down to the paintings of the Old Country and shelves lined with homemade limoncello. And, for the crowd of diplomats and intellectuals who flock here, these anything-but-trendy environs are precisely the draw.

Though the food is rustic at its core, presentation is nothing if not elegant; and Chef Luigi Diotaiuti's dedication to ingredients has been recognized by DC Slow Food. Menu highlights include toothsome pappardelle tossed with sliced portobello mushrooms in a deliciously savory sauce, as well as grilled fish, lamb chops, and roast chicken. Whatever you choose, be sure to save room for the namesake—and just right—tiramisu.

◼ 2014 P St. NW (bet. Hopkins & 20th Sts.)
🚇 Dupont Circle
☏ (202) 467-4466 — **WEB:** www.altiramisu.com
◼ Lunch Mon – Fri   Dinner nightly   **PRICE: $$**

AMBAR 🍴

Balkan

✗ | 🍸 ⛱ 🍽   **MAP:** 4-C2

Come armed with an appetite, as there are over 40 small plates and the reasonably priced "Balkan Experience" offers unlimited servings. Though this cuisine is known to be hearty, the kitchen isn't heavy-handed and presents an enticing lineup.

The ćevapi piles smoky, succulent minced beef and pork kebabs onto a thin slice of charred flatbread and christens it with a swipe of kajmak, a funky sour Balkan cheese. Pita sa sirom takes impossibly paper-thin phyllo and layers it with a crumbly, salty cheese and egg filling. The parade of cured meats, flatbreads, salads, and sausages should all be washed down with rakia, a classic spirit made from quince or plum. Just in case you thought it would be easy to pick, there are more than 30 varieties on the menu.

■ 523 8th St. SE (bet. E & G Sts.)
🚇 Eastern Market
📞 (202) 813-3039 — **WEB:** www.ambarrestaurant.com
■ Lunch & dinner daily   **PRICE:** $$

ANXO 🍴

Basque

✗ | 🍺 ⛱ 🍽   **MAP:** 2-D4

This Cider House rules. Anxo focuses on cider and small plates hailing from Spain's Basque region. Downstairs, the pintxos bar and wood cask lend a fun, traditional flair, while upstairs has a raw, industrial-meets-rustic appearance. And speaking of which, pintxos (an offering of bite-sized tapas) may include marinated mussels, bacalao fritters, oyster mushroom-stuffed piquillos, chistorra sausage and aged Manchego among others. The local heirloom red and yellow tomato salad with shaved onion and balsamic vinegar is simply delicious. Stuffed txipiron (squid) is set over caramelized onions, while the Onaga red snapper escabeche, grilled à la plancha, rests in a deliciously tart marinade.

Not into cider? Basque wines, sherries, and vermouths do the trick.

■ 300 Florida Ave. NW (at 3rd St.)
🚇 Shaw-Howard U
📞 (202) 986-3795 — **WEB:** www.anxodc.com
■ Lunch Sat – Sun   Dinner nightly   **PRICE:** $$

BAD SAINT 😋

Filipino

🍴

You'll need the patience of a saint to dine here as they don't take reservations and have no phone to prove the point; but good things do come to those who wait. Once inside, the mood is appealingly boisterous; and seats are in the thick of it all—near the tiny kitchen. The chef isn't letting his fame go to his head and he's still upping his game, creating a variety of Filipino adobos and other flavor-packed dynamo dishes.

Sisig arrives on a sizzling plate with chopped pork jowl and chilies, along with a raw egg cracked in the center for hot and creamy goodness. Then dig into kinilaw na pugita, a refreshing ceviche-style dish. Luckily, deep-fried apples nestled inside spring roll wrappers make for a tasty finish, as they're the only option for dessert!

🔲 3226 11th St. NW (bet. Kenyon & Lamont Sts.)

🔗 N/A — **WEB:** www.badsaintdc.com

🔲 Dinner Wed – Mon

PRICE: $$

BIDWELL 😋

American

🍴 | ♿ 🛋

You will indeed fare well at Bidwell. Tucked inside Union Market, it checks all of the boxes for a modern hot spot. Trendy, industrial-chic design (exposed air ducts, rough concrete walls) in the up-and-coming NoMa hood? Yes. Hipster-packed bar? Got it. Buzzworthy food? Indeed. Bidwell takes the farm-to-table trend and tops it—quite literally—since the rooftop garden supplies much of the kitchen's produce.

The menu may read classic, but this chef is no simpleton. Calamari stuffed with shrimp, spicy chorizo, and served over piquillo pepper purée really goes for the gusto. Herb-roasted chicken is seared to a golden-brown, crispy delight, and when paired with heartbreakingly tender braised kale and crunchy, salty potatoes, it's positively perfect.

🔲 1309 5th St. NE (in Union Market)

🔳 NoMa-Gallaudet U

🔗 (202) 547-0172 — **WEB:** www.bidwelldc.com

🔲 Lunch & dinner Tue – Sun

PRICE: $$

THE BIRD 🍴

Contemporary

XX | 🪑 | 🛋️

Most everyone loves chicken, but The Bird turns something that seems like a safe bet into a very worthy dinner. Meals commence with a wink to the menu's celebration of poultry by offering diners a complimentary bowl of "bird seed"—a savory mix of pepitas, sunflower seeds, and raisins. The humble chicken reaches for new heights here, finding global influence in the crunchy, sweet, and spicy Korean wings sprinkled with cilantro; grilled chicken draped in bright red peri-peri sauce; or duck meatballs in tomato curry. Count on the brunch menu to highlight myriad egg creations.

Located near Logan Circle, the bi-level space is lively and festooned with custom works from local artists. If pork is more your style though, try sibling restaurant, The Pig.

🔲 1337 11th St. NW (at O St.)
🚇 Mt Vernon Sq
📞 (202) 518-3609 — **WEB:** www.thebirddc.com
🔲 Lunch Sat – Sun   Dinner nightly   PRICE: $$

BLACKSALT 🍴

Seafood

XX | 🛋️

Fried, wood-grilled, simmered, steamed, or raw. No, it's not a line from Forrest Gump. As long as it swims, you can have it any way you want it at BlackSalt. It's all fish, all the time at this fish market-cum-restaurant in Palisades. There is a lively, bistro vibe here, where the bar is made for a cocktail and a platter of freshly shucked oysters; while private booths appeal to a sophisticated, older crowd.

The concise menu trawls coast to continent for inspiration, with dishes such as fried Ipswich clams and fish tacos to Provençal stew. Bigeye tuna tartare is silky; and potato-crusted skate wing is topped with a fragrant brown butter-mustard vinaigrette.

Hit the market on the way out for gourmet items to stock the pantry and soups to fill the freezer.

🔲 4883 MacArthur Blvd. (bet. U & V Sts.)
📞 (202) 342-9101 — **WEB:** www.blacksaltrestaurant.com
🔲 Lunch & dinner daily   PRICE: $$

BLUE DUCK TAVERN ✿
American

XxX | 🍸 ♿ 🏖 ⊡ 🛋 📭 🛎

Simply put, Blue Duck Tavern will have you at hello. Set within the Park Hyatt, this upscale American tavern makes a dazzling first impression with its 25-foot entry doors, floor-to-ceiling windows, walnut wood seating, and highly coveted glass-enclosed booths. (And if that doesn't have you swooning, the dessert station, piled high with tempting treats, certainly will.) Whether seated in the plush dining room or expansive lounge—which features a totally separate cheese and charcuterie-focused menu—the gorgeous space and its well-to-do crowd are the epitome of casual sophistication.

At the center of the massive open kitchen sits a wood-burning oven, a behemoth centerpiece that turns out everything from fragrant, crusty bread to oven-fired Kansas Prime steak with Worcestershire gastrique. The menu spotlights such East Coast delicacies as cider-braised lamb shank from Shenandoah, VA; roasted duck breast from Hudson Valley, NY; and brown-butter roasted grouper from Florida.

In a unique twist, many of the dishes—from perfectly cooked Maine scallops with a mild horseradish jus to pan-roasted rock fish with spot-on dirty rice—are served not on plates, but in top-quality cookware.

🟦 1201 24th St. NW (bet. M & N Sts.)
🚇 Foggy Bottom-GWU
📞 (202) 419-6755 — **WEB:** www.blueducktavern.com
🟦 Lunch & dinner daily

PRICE: $$$

BOMBAY CLUB 🍴

Indian

XX   **MAP:** 1-C4

A fixture on the DC scene since Bush senior was in office, this Penn Quarter stalwart, owned by the affable Ashok Bajaj, still functions as a club for politicians and Beltway insiders. Polished and sophisticated with just a hint of spice, Bombay Club's environs are decidedly grown-up and the service appropriately white-glove.

If you can take your eyes off the senator snuggled into the half-moon banquette, the elegant Indian food doesn't disappoint. Tender, velvety squid is marked by a wildly flavorful combination of fennel and anise that dances on the tongue. Saag gosht's rich mustard greens and well-spiced lamb are a pleasant surprise, while the gulab jamun, milk dumplings with rose syrup and cardamom ice cream, makes a light and balanced finish.

■ 815 Connecticut Ave. NW (bet. H & I Sts.)
🚇 Farragut West
🕾 (202) 659-3727 — **WEB:** www.bombayclubdc.com
■ Lunch Sun – Fri   Dinner nightly   **PRICE:** $$$

BOQUERIA 😊

Spanish

XX | 🏠 🛋   **MAP:** 1-B2

Boqueria may be an import from New York City, but the flavor is straight up Spain. This slightly creaky row home belies the stylish and modern interior. Head upstairs for a tête-à-tête, while the main level's bar displaying meats and cheeses whets the appetite for what's to come. And what is to come? Tapas, tapas, and more tapas. Sure, there are salads and sandwiches, but with all-day small plates tempting you, why diverge?

The offerings are familiar, with plenty of Spanish classics (croquetas, those fried fritters of gooey deliciousness, for one), but contemporary creations make their mark. Colorado lamb meatballs in a rich tomato sauce with sheep's milk cheese are spot on, while pulpo a la plancha over olive oil-mashed potatoes delivers a pop of flavor.

■ 1837 M St. NW (at 19th St.)
🚇 Farragut North
🕾 (202) 558-9545 — **WEB:** www.boqueriadc.com
■ Lunch & dinner daily   **PRICE:** $$

17

BOURBON STEAK ¶○

Steakhouse

✗✗ | 器 ⅃ ⊡ ♨

It's snuggled inside the sophisticated Four Seasons Hotel, so expect a moneyed crowd of executives and deep-pocketed locals who come here to dine on pricey dry aged and grass fed steaks and burgers. This Michael Mina steakhouse nails the modern masculine demeanor with its earth-toned palette and chocolate leather-inlaid tables. At lunch, the vibe is all business, while nighttime brings a scene-y crowd with a trendier take.

Dig right in to the fresh-from-the-oven rolls while pondering their various cuts of meat. There are a few concessions (Korean barbecue salmon burger, anyone?), but it's really all about the cow. Duck-fat fries accessorize nicely, but the kitchen saves the best for last. Smoked s'mores are a creative rejiggering of the campsite favorite.

■ 2800 Pennsylvania Ave. NW (bet. 28th & 29th Sts.)
🚇 Foggy Bottom-GWU
✆ (202) 944-2026 — **WEB:** www.bourbonsteakdc.com
■ Lunch Mon – Fri Dinner nightly   **PRICE: $$$$**

CAVA MEZZE ¶○

Greek

✗ | ♨

It turns out that you can be all things to all people, at least at Cava Mezze. This place manages to lure the post-work crowd who come to down drinks and talk shop. Yet this casual Greek restaurant with palatable prices is also popular among families with young children.

There is a long list of shareable plates, plus seafood, meat and pasta. Additionally, quality ingredients sourced from area farms enhance simple preparations. While most of these honor the Greek standards (for instance, spanakopita is revved up by thick, creamy Greek yogurt and tender, buttery lamb chops are accompanied by fluffy fries), the kitchen also challenges convention. If that's not enough, it even delivers a few Med-influenced riffs—perhaps lamb sliders and orzo mac n cheese?

■ 527 8th St. SE (bet. E & G Sts.)
🚇 Eastern Market
✆ (202) 543-9090 — **WEB:** www.cavamezze.com
■ Lunch Tue – Sun Dinner nightly   **PRICE: $$**

CHERCHER 😊

Ethiopian

✗   **MAP:** 3-A1

There are some restaurants that feed more than just an appetite and Chercher is one of them. Set on the second floor of a townhouse just outside Little Ethiopia, this tidy jewel may have the bright walls and exposed brick so often seen in mom-and-pop spots, but rest assured that it delivers more than just a spicy stew with a home-kitchen feel.

Expect authentic items native to the culturally rich region of the Chercher Mountains. Rip off a piece of the cool and lacy injera and then dig into the lamb wat, a tender stew fueled by the fiery notes of berbere. Simmered vegetables add a welcome dose of earthy flavor on the side, but wait, what's that over there? It's the under-the-radar and off-the-menu dishes that lure expats with bated breath.

🔲 1334 9th St. NW (bet. N & O Sts.)
🔲 Mt Vernon Sq
☏ (202) 299-9703 — **WEB:** www.chercherrestaurant.com
🔲 Lunch & dinner daily   **PRICE:** 🍸

CHINA CHILCANO 😊

Peruvian

✗✗ | 🍸 ♿ 🏛 🔪 🧼   **MAP:** 3-B4

Bring a pile of friends and keep the piscos coming at this José Andrés hot spot, where a vibrant décor and bold, flavorful cuisine are the antidote to humdrum. China Chilcano is playfulness personified, and this is evident even in their restrooms, where guests scribble on the chalkboard-painted walls.

Chinese-style steamed dumplings with rocoto chili-accented dipping sauce or hamachi served in a pool of slightly spicy aji amarillo leche de tigre reflect Peru's strong Chinese and Japanese cultural influences. Causa limena is layer after delicious layer of classic Peruvian flavors, albeit in an elegantly plated presentation. The aji rocoto has a distinctly fruity essence blended with a garlicky goodness that makes everything it touches turn to gold.

🔲 416 7th St. NW (bet. D & E Sts.)
🔲 Archives
☏ (202) 783-0941 — **WEB:** www.chinachilcano.com
🔲 Lunch & dinner daily   **PRICE:** $$

CONVIVIAL 🍴

French

XX | ⛱

Truth be told, Convivial excels in all areas. It scores major points for its location, anchoring the base of City Market at O in the up-and-coming Shaw neighborhood; ranks high on style with its clean, rustic-modern aesthetic; and boasts service so downright relaxed, the servers wear jeans and sneakers. But the real reason customers keep coming back to this energetic hot spot is most certainly for the food: bold and playful takes on the tried-and-true that are made for sharing.

Popular with young professionals, families, and academics from nearby Howard University, the whimsical, new-meets-old menu marries French and American cuisine. Think garlicky, deep-fried escargots in a blanket, fried chicken coq au vin, or Chesapeake blue catfish bouillabaisse.

    801 O St. NW (bet. 8th & 9th Sts.)
    Mt Vernon Sq
    (202) 525-2870 — **WEB:** www.convivialdc.com
    Lunch Sat – Sun   Dinner nightly   **PRICE: $$**

DAIKAYA 🍴

Japanese

X | ♿

There are restaurants where soaking in the atmosphere is part of the experience, and then there's Daikaya. This no-reservations ramen shop is bursting at the seams (though the izakaya upstairs is an acceptable consolation prize if the wait downstairs is interminable). The unfussy space is filled with communal tables and booths, but the counter offers an unbeatable view of the hustle and bustle.

Loud pop and rap music set the tone here, where you're expected to order, slurp, and move on. There are just five types of ramen: shio, shoyu, mugi-miso (barley miso), spicy miso, and vegetable (100% vegan), but the bowls can also be customized—slightly—with the addition of extra toppings or noodles. If you want chicken-based ramen, check out nearby sib, Bantam King.

    705 6th St. NW (at G St.)
    Gallery Pl-Chinatown
    (202) 589-1600 — **WEB:** www.daikaya.com
    Lunch & dinner daily   **PRICE:** 🍴

THE DABNEY ✿

American

🍴 | 🍸 ♿ 🛖

MAP: 3-A1

Your mother warned you about walking down dark alleys, but shush her voice in your head and traipse down Blagden Alley to The Dabney. It's like finding the end of the rainbow—make your way inside to discover a chic farmhouse-style interior, boasting an open kitchen, wood-fired oven, as well as a young, eclectic and well-dressed crowd. And then there is the food, which is nothing short of stellar.

In fact, Chef Jeremiah Langhorne—who interned at Noma and cooked at McCrady's in Charleston—is the patriarch here. As if that weren't enough, this Virginia native is the king of mid-Atlantic fish, local dairy, creamy grits, and other classic American ingredients.

This chef-driven menu is a successful marriage of traditional and contemporary flavors. If the likes of pan-fried Chesapeake catfish, dressed up with a mildly spicy hot sauce and served with calypso beans, bacon, wilted spinach, and brown butter foam ring a bell, then you're starting to get the picture. Flame-kissed from the grill and garnished with fried shallot rings, soy, and chili, grilled bok choy is far from a side dish. A buttermilk pie crowned with strawberry jam and yogurt foam makes for a divine finish.

🟦 122 Blagden Alley NW (bet. M & N Sts.)
🟦 Mt Vernon Sq
📞 (202) 450-1015 — **WEB:** www.thedabney.com
🟦 Dinner Tue – Sun

PRICE: $$

DAS 😋
Ethiopian

✕✕ | ⬭

Nestled inside a classic Georgetown townhouse, Das is a haven of soothing colors and lush fabrics. Great care has gone into its styling, and the warm, generous spirit of the staff ensures that the entire experience is every bit as pleasant and refined.

The impressive menu runs the gamut from traditional Ethiopian cuisine to dishes that have the potential to take even the most seasoned and ambitious palate by surprise. A basket filled with injera—a spongy and sour bread that serves as both chaser and utensil—is never-ending. For a meal that won't disappoint, order the chicken and beef combination sampler. Then use rolls of that delicious injera to dig into mouthful after flavorful mouthful of surprisingly varied textures and degrees of heat.

■ 1201 28th St. NW (at M St.)
🚇 Foggy Bottom-GWU
✆ (202) 333-4710 — **WEB:** www.dasethiopian.com
■ Lunch & dinner daily

PRICE: $$

DBGB KITCHEN AND BAR 🍴
French

✕✕ | 🍹 🍺 ♿ ⛩ ⬭ 🛋 📋

DBGB Kitchen and Bar's City Center locale may rub shoulders with the likes of Hermès and Louis Vuitton, but this light-filled French restaurant maintains a relaxed elegance with tile floors, dark wood furnishings, and orb pendant lights. It's the kind of place where local politicos and dealmakers come to dish, drink, and dine.

The menu is varied, but you'll want to skip the ambitious Americanized cuisine and head straight for the house-made sausages and traditional French selections: pan-roasted salmon is well-seasoned and crispy alongside an eye-pleasing vegetable assortment topped with crumbled bacon. Meanwhile, the flaky lemon tart, packed with thick lemon curd and accompanied by a quenelle of blood orange sorbet, makes for a truly satisfying finale.

■ 931 H St. NW (bet. 9th & 10th Sts.)
🚇 Gallery Pl-Chinatown
✆ (202) 695-7660 — **WEB:** www.dbgb.com
■ Lunch & dinner daily

PRICE: $$

DECANTER ∥○

Mediterranean

XxX | 🍸 ♿ 🖼 🛋 🖥   **MAP:** 1-C3

Decanter is the latest incarnation of the St. Regis Hotel's signature restaurant, and it reflects the traditional elegance of this Beaux-Arts beauty while punctuating the space with a hint of contemporary panache. Imagine soaring ceilings and sleek dark wood paneling, complemented by ivory leather and polished chrome seating.

The talented and internationally-trained team is led by Spanish-born chef, Javier Cuesta Muñoz, whose kitchen routinely presents a globally inspired menu prepared with confidence. Risotto studded with fresh seafood and fava beans is artfully plated, echoing the elegant background and setting an impressive tone. Then look forward to a rack of tender, juicy Colorado lamb, tailed by parsnip dumplings and enhanced by huckleberry sauce.

■ 923 16th St. NW (at K St.)
🚇 Farragut North
✆ (202) 509-8000 — **WEB:** www.decanterdc.com
■ Lunch Mon – Fri Dinner Tue – Sat   **PRICE: $$$$**

DEL CAMPO ∥○

Latin American

XX | 🏠 🖼 🛋 🖥   **MAP:** 3-B2

Del Campo brings the spirit and style of la estancia to this burgeoning Arts district, though you'll want to resist the urge to judge a book by its cover when visiting. Its rather bland façade belies a refined-rustic interior.

It's all smoke and meat at this Latin American steakhouse, where Chef Victor Albisu (who trained at Le Cordon Bleu in Paris) delivers straight-up South American flavor. Asado dominates the kitchen's cooking style, and the smoke imparts an intriguing complexity to everything—even the olive oil accompanied by pillowy chapa bread. Glistening cubes of tuna tartare are tucked inside a jar that swirls with smoke and is opened ceremoniously by a well-attired waiter, while the perfectly charred skirt steak is nothing less than butter-soft.

■ 777 I St. NW (bet. 7th & 9th Sts.)
🚇 Gallery Pl-Chinatown
✆ (202) 289-7377 — **WEB:** www.delcampodc.com
■ Lunch & dinner daily   **PRICE: $$$**

DGS DELICATESSEN 🍴

Deli

🍴 | ♿ 📠

DGS Delicatessen's corned beef, potato latkes, and braised brisket are so good that bubbes everywhere are crying into their matzo ball soup. Why trek to grandma's when DGS is right off Dupont Circle? White tile work, wood tabletops, and aluminum chairs lend a retro-but-updated look to this bright and airy restaurant that positively buzzes with a local business crowd.

Spoon up the salty goodness of smoked and cured fish before tucking into a never-fail deli sandwich. Thick, warm pastrami with a peppery crust and glistening with silky fat is layered on sliced rye for a simple, but oh-so-good meal. Shareable plates and heartier main courses (chicken schnitzel) will have you swearing off that diet till tomorrow. Besides, aren't you too thin anyway?

🔲 1317 Connecticut Ave. NW (bet. Dupont Cir. & N St.)
🚇 Dupont Circle
📞 (202) 293-4400 — **WEB:** www.dgsdelicatessen.com
🔲 Lunch & dinner daily

PRICE: $$

THE DINER 🍴

American

🍴 | 🏠 📠 📠

Nothing replaces a good diner. Where else can you tuck into a plate of bacon-wrapped meatloaf at 2:00 A.M.? The Diner is open 24/7 and its frenetic kitchen is always abuzz. Start off with a really good cup of Counter Culture coffee or if you're feeling more hair of the dog, a Bloody Mary.

It's not just standard diner fare here, where breakfast specials like bread pudding-French toast and tofu scramble with house-made salsa lean gourmet. Nursing a hangover? Straight-up comfort food is what they do best. Order the biscuit and gravy, highlighting a flaky house-made biscuit slathered in creamy sauce with sweet Italian sausage—it's a decadent way to start the day. Finally, sip on a cookies-and-cream milkshake, best enjoyed atop a red vinyl stool at the counter.

🔲 2453 18th St. NW (bet. Columbia & Belmont Rds.)
🚇 Woodley Park
📞 (202) 232-8800 — **WEB:** www.dinerdc.com
🔲 Lunch & dinner daily

PRICE: 💰

DISTRICT COMMONS 🍴

American

XX | 🍺 ♿ 🍽 🖥 🛋 ✋　　　　　**MAP:** 1-A3

Sometimes you want a place that crosses all of its t's without a lot of drama—and District Commons, set on a bright corner, hits the spot with its extensive drinks list, impressive beer selection, and comprehensive menu of eats. A U-shaped concrete bar dominates the scene, while wood-plank flooring, bare wood tables, and slanted concrete columns come together in a minimalist, slightly masculine look that's cool, comfortable, and broadly appealing.

The kitchen turns out American dishes, many with Southern influences, such as shrimp and grits or duck with sweet potato hash. Their strength is in the classics, so order one of the burgers, crispy hearth-baked flatbreads, or steamed mussels, before digging into a slice of the fudgy Boston cream pie for dessert.

■ 2200 Pennsylvania Ave. NW (at Washington Circle)
🚇 Foggy Bottom-GWU
📞 (202) 587-8277 — **WEB:** www.districtcommonsdc.com
■ Lunch & dinner daily　　　　　**PRICE:** $$

DOI MOI 😀

Asian

XX | ♿ 🍽 🖥　　　　　**MAP:** 2-B4

Set on a corner and flooded with sunshine, Doi Moi's interior is defined by its light, bright and mostly white modern look. Seating is limited to a long, expansive counter facing the exhibition kitchen, as well as two dining areas with sleek tables framed by simple blonde wood chairs.

The restaurant's minimalist interior belies the flavor-packed riot of its food. The kitchen turns out spicy and bold Southeast Asian dishes, most with a heavy Thai bent. House-made Isaan-style pork sausage, salty-sweet and smoky in flavor, is expertly paired with pungent pickled vegetables and chilies. Served in a deliciously spiced and creamy coconut curry, the khao soi braised chicken is fall-off-the-bone tender and placed atop toothsome egg noodles.

■ 1800 14th St. NW (at S St.)
🚇 U St
📞 (202) 733-5131 — **WEB:** www.doimoidc.com
■ Dinner nightly　　　　　**PRICE:** $$

DUE SOUTH 🍴

Southern

✗✗ | 🍺 ♿ 🏠 ⛵

Set in the Lumber Shed building smack dab in the middle of the Yards Park, Due South is bright and airy with high ceilings and walls of windows. But the wraparound patio with its stellar views of the park and river is the place to be.

This kitchen's compass certainly points south and smoked meats are ever-present, but there's nothing simple about their prettied-up Southern-style cooking, enhanced with seasonal produce. Kale and heirloom tomatoes take the lead out of typically heavy shrimp and grits, while the Brunswick stew is particularly flavorful. If the hanger steak with broccoli rabe feels a little too—well, northern—take refuge in a slice of pie or cobbler. Beers by the draft or bottle are plentiful, but check the rotating list of specialty brews.

■ 301 Water St. SE (at 3rd St.)
🚇 Navy Yard-Ballpark
✆ (202) 479-4616 — **WEB:** www.duesouthdc.com
■ Lunch & dinner daily   **PRICE:** $$

EATBAR 🍴

Gastropub

✗ | 🍇 🍺 ♿ ⛵

Where do you go when you want to throw back a few beers, listen to good tunes and catch up with pals? Eatbar. This casual spot is like your living room, only with better food (and a way-cool jukebox). It's all about the sharing economy here, where small plates rule the roost. The beer list is vast and the wine selection surprises with lesser known finds.

Small-batch charcuterie and whole animal butchery are passions of the chef, so the menu is meat-driven, but right sizing keeps portions in check. The carte is whimsically categorized so while "bready things" bring a summer tomato tartine with ricotta, "beasty things" unveil a Cotechino burger enriched with tomato aïoli and melted cheese. Seal the deal with "sweet things" like lemon-scented ricotta donuts.

■ 415 8th St. SE (bet. D & E Sts.)
🚇 Eastern Market
✆ (202) 847-4827 — **WEB:** www.eat-bar.com
■ Lunch Sat – Sun   Dinner nightly   **PRICE:** $$

ESPITA MEZCALERIA 🍴

Mexican

X | 🍸 ♿ 🛏

MAP: 3-A1

The name is the first sign that this place takes its mezcal seriously. Step inside, where dark woods, concrete floors, and steel accents vibe industrial and you'll find shelves lined with the elixir. The selection is eye-popping and there are even certified Master mezcaliers on staff, so prepare to go in late tomorrow and kick back with a flight. That said, Espita Mezcaleria is so much more than just a watering hole.

The kitchen turns out tasty Southern Mexican items—think tortas and tacos at lunch and seven types of house-made mole and other heartier entrées for dinner. Tender, shredded short rib-topped griddled sopes are moist and nutty, while the flaky grilled tilapia-packed tacos drizzled with a creamy chipotle-mayo are...one word...sensational.

◼ 1250 9th St. NW (at N St.)
🚇 Mt Vernon Sq
🕿 (202) 621-9695 — **WEB:** www.espitadc.com
◼ Lunch & dinner daily

PRICE: $$

ESTADIO 🍴

Spanish

XX | 🍸 ♿ 🛏

MAP: 1-D1

With its stone-accented walls, chunky wood furnishings, and poured concrete bar studded with Moorish tile, Estadio, or "stadium," plays up its Spanish influences. It's no surprise then that the focus is on tapas, but these unusual combinations and preparations offer a pleasant twist on tradition.

Golden-brown jamón croquetas are amped up with pickled cucumber; fava bean and almond spread is a thick and creamy snack; and sizzling squid a la plancha is drizzled with a citrusy salsa verde. Wash it all down with a glass of wine from Spain, Portugal, and the Canary Islands; a cocktail mixed with house-made tonics; or even a slushito—an icy blend of grapefruit, Bourbon, and amontillado, designed to counteract a hot summer's night.

◼ 1520 14th St. NW (at Church St.)
🕿 (202) 319-1404 — **WEB:** www.estadio-dc.com
◼ Lunch Fri – Sun   Dinner nightly

PRICE: $$

ETHIOPIC ¶◯
Ethiopian

✗ | ⛱

With its large windows, bustling energy, and brightly hued interior, Ethiopic is an ideal fit for the melting pot that is H Street. Though minimalist, the dining room's bare tables are juxtaposed with pops of color from decorative wall hangings and other art.

This family-run spot turns out classic, well-made dishes with complex flavors, and the menu is a veritable treasure trove for vegetarians. Tibs, a marinated beef or lamb dish served with sautéed vegetables, delivers a kick of heat; while the slowly simmered beef in the sega key wot proves that good things do come to those who wait. Of course, everything comes with the obligatory injera, thicker here than usual, and no meal is complete without a cup of that seriously rich Ethiopian coffee.

◼ 401 H St. NE (at 4th St.)
◻ Union Station
✆ (202) 675-2066 — **WEB:** www.ethiopicrestaurant.com
◼ Lunch Fri – Sun   Dinner Tue – Sun
                                         PRICE: $$

FIOLA MARE ¶◯
Seafood

✗✗✗ | 🍸 ⛱ 🖥 🛋 🍽

Fact: Fiola Mare has a primo location. Resting right at the edge of the Potomac River, the setting hugs the river so every table comes with a view. It's part of the collection of restaurants run by Fabio Trabocchi, and like its name, this kitchen is seafood driven with Italian overtones.

Some dishes try too hard—the burrata has far too many competing flavors—but simple grilled seafood is always a good choice. Of course, there is no going wrong with dessert, specifically the chocolate soufflé crostata. While it may require a wait, your patience will be rewarded after one bite of the bittersweet Valrhona chocolate cremosa, baked to order and fluffy-as-air with a toasted hazelnut crust. And though it needs no further gussying up, it is served with torrone gelato and truffle honey.

◼ 3050 K St. NW, Ste. 101 (at 31st St.)
◻ Foggy Bottom-GWU
✆ (202) 628-0065 — **WEB:** www.fiolamaredc.com
◼ Lunch Tue – Sun   Dinner nightly
                                         PRICE: $$$

FIOLA ✿
Italian

XX | ✿ ♿ ☂ ⬚ 🖐

Polished and professional with an upscale setting made for brokering deals, Fiola is just what the politician ordered. Its central location near the Archives makes it a go-to for the power crowd, and the bar is perfect for blowing off steam after a busy day of debating.

Thanks to truly sophisticated cuisine, the somewhat stiff environs and overly scripted staff are soon forgiven—and despite its traditional feel, the menu actually allows for flexibility with the ability to craft your own prix-fixe in addition to a tasting menu.

The chef's impressive cooking style is both ultra-luxurious and Italian-influenced, with a highly stylized bent to boot. Porcini cappuccino, a flan studded with foie gras, is proof positive that decadence reigns, while polenta with a foamy parmesan and gorgonzola dolce fonduta and black truffle is subtly elegant. Delicately prepared lobster wrapped in thin ravioli rests in a fragrant ginger- and chive-scented lobster nage; and chestnut-layered tiramisu topped with chestnut granita is a creative reboot.

As for the wine list? As one would expect, it's showy, littered with big names, and curated for those with sizeable expense accounts and companions to impress.

▪ 601 Pennsylvania Ave. NW (entrance on Indiana Ave.)
▪ Archives
✆ (202) 628-2888 — **WEB:** www.fioladc.com
▪ Lunch Mon – Fri Dinner nightly   **PRICE: $$$$**

GARRISON 🍴

American

✕✕ | 🚤 ᴀ   **MAP: 4-C2**

Despite the heavy competition in its bustling Barracks Row location, Garrison stands apart with its farm-fresh food and its modern-rustic good looks. The brick patio, lined with flowering plants and herbs, makes a good first impression, and heat lamps extend the life of alfresco dining. Inside, abundant wood defines the look, which subscribes to the Scandinavian, less-is-more school of thought.

Area farms dictate the menu, but for hyper-seasonal selections, note the handwritten daily specials. The cooking style is ramped up American: smoke-infused potatoes are balanced by a pungent ramp aïoli; and green chickpea-crusted Chesapeake blue catfish is matched with a rhubarb coulis. Strawberry short cake parfait is like springtime in a glass.

◾ 524 8th St. SE (bet. E & G Sts.)
🚇 Eastern Market
📞 (202) 506-2445 — **WEB:** www.garrisondc.com
◾ Lunch Sun Dinner Tue – Sun   **PRICE: $$**

GHIBELLINA 🍴

Italian

✕ | ♿ 🚤 ᴀ   **MAP: 1-D1**

Ghibellina's marble bar is a favorite hangout, but don't let the cocktail-swilling patrons steer you away, since this kitchen gives its bar a serious run. Dark wood floors, iron accents, and exposed brick are a nod to the Old World, while the front sidewalk patio is a top people-watching spot.

Lunch is largely focused on salads and knockout pizzas. Ramp pizza reveals a delightful interplay between zingy, garlicky-onion ramps and creamy cheeses, including crumbled ricotta and fior di latte. Dinner expands to include antipasti, pastas (like bucatini alle vongole), and mains (like pollo al mattone or chicken under a brick). It's a linger-a-little-longer kind of place, so order dessert. The affogato al caffe's gelato with robust espresso is a nice finish.

◾ 1610 14th St. NW (bet. Corcoran & Q Sts.)
🚇 U St
📞 (202) 803-2389 — **WEB:** www.ghibellina.com
◾ Lunch Wed – Sun Dinner nightly   **PRICE: $$**

HANK'S OYSTER BAR 🍴

Seafood

✗ | ♿ 🏠 🍷

MAP: 1-C1

The original of three locations, Hank's Oyster Bar promises a good time and a full stomach. Snag a seat on the spacious front patio or opt for a table indoors where bottles of malt vinegar and Old Bay seasoning are a sign of things to come.

Meals begin with a bowl of humble Goldfish cheese crackers, and then prepare yourself for a sea, ahem, of dishes. Feast on platters of raw bar beauties to bowls of steaming chowder to oysters any way you want 'em (Hog Island style involves dunking in a tangy lemon-garlic-Tabasco-butter sauce, a sprinkling of breadcrumbs and shredded cheese, and broiling until caramelized!). Of course, lobster rolls and crab cake sandwiches with Old Bay-seasoned fries are positively Proustian, conjuring up days at the beach from years past.

▪ 1624 Q St. NW (bet. 16th & 17th Sts.)
▪ Dupont Circle
✆ (202) 462-4265 — **WEB:** www.hanksoysterbar.com
▪ Lunch & dinner daily

PRICE: $$

HAZEL 😀

Fusion

✗✗ | 🍺 ♿ 🏠 🍷

MAP: 2-C4

Tucked into D.C.'s hip Shaw neighborhood, this charmer is low-lit and cozy by evening, with Sunday brunch offering a brighter ambience care of jumbo windows and an outdoor patio. Dishes are a mash-up of ingredients from around the world, tied together with an East Asian slant—a vision deftly translated by a kitchen skilled enough to weave disparate ingredients into a fun, cohesive menu.

The shareable plates are divided into simple categories: vegetables, breads, fish, and meat. Crispy tofu arrives perfectly creamy in the center, topped with a shiitake mushroom sauce and Sichuan pepper; while succulent cuttlefish bokkeum is stir-fried with pickled green onion, charred scallion, and spirals of carrots, then laced with Korean red pepper glaze.

▪ 808 V St. NW (bet. 8th & 9th Sts.)
▪ Shaw-Howard U
✆ (202) 847-4980 — **WEB:** www.hazelrestaurant.com
▪ Lunch Sun   Dinner nightly

PRICE: $$

HIMITSU 🍴

Asian

✕ | 🍸

MAP: 2-C1

Take a small space, a cool staff, and wildly creative kitchen and what do you get? Himitsu, naturally. Perhaps it should come as no surprise that it has garnered so much buzz as it is exceedingly more fun than your average spot, and ergo, another notch in the belt of DC's dining scene.

Don't bother Googling—there is no phone and they don't take reservations. But if you're lucky (or patient) enough to snag a seat at the bar or one of the snug tables, you'll find a fun, inventive menu that takes inspiration from, well, everywhere. While the cooking is Asian in the broadest sense of the word (read: Japanese-inspired rolls and small plates like Korean fried chicken or fish curry), other items could benefit from more focus. Regardless, the crowds keep coming.

■ 828 Upshur St. NW (bet. 8th & 9th Sts.)
✆ N/A — **WEB:** www.himitsudc.com
■ Dinner Tue – Sat

PRICE: $$

HONEYSUCKLE 🍴

American

✕✕✕ | 🍽 🖋

MAP: 1-B2

Planted in Vidalia's original home turf and run by an alum of the onion-monikered restaurant, it's safe to say Honeysuckle is all about keeping it in the family—and that's a good thing. Inside, bold touches include artwork inspired by the chef's tattoos, while white tablecloths prevent it from looking too trendy.

Tuck into the bread basket, a delicious gesture filled with a buttery roll studded with ham and cheddar cheese; sweet zucchini bread; and a hearty beer roll. The menu leans American, but the chef's love affair with all things Nordic means items such as slow-roasted Icelandic cod are worth ordering. Buttery veal sweetbreads tucked inside a pastry shell and finished with a béarnaise pudding sauce are decidedly delicious—if a touch decadent.

■ 1990 M St. NW (bet. 19th & 20th Sts.)
🚇 Farragut North
✆ (202) 659-1990 — **WEB:** www.honeysuckledc.com
■ Lunch Wed – Fri   Dinner nightly

PRICE: $$$

INDIGO 🍴

Indian

🍴 | ⛱

MAP: 8-A3

It's yellow, not the telltale blue of its name, that defines this sunny Indian restaurant. Located in a cheerful yellow house with a patio full of colorful picnic tables, Indigo is far from fancy (it's largely self-service and food is served in disposable containers). But, how can you not adore a place where love notes from customers cover the walls?

Indian expats and residents line up for classic comfort food from the sub-continent, such as spicy chicken masala and melt-in-your-mouth-tender bone-in goat curry. Even side dishes are elevated here—daal is packed with smoky flavor and doused in a cardamom-scented sauce, while paneer paratha (flatbread stuffed with cheese, onion, chopped red chilies, and cilantro) is especially fluffy and fantastic.

◼ 243 K St. NE (at 3rd St.)
🚇 NoMa-Gallaudet U
📞 (202) 544-4777 — **WEB:** www.indigowdc.com
◼ Lunch Mon – Fri   Dinner Mon – Sat

PRICE: 🥜

INDIQUE 🍴

Indian

🍴🍴 | 🍸 ♿ 🛋

MAP: 6-C1

The name—no kidding—sure sums this spot up. Make your way inside only to discover that this bi-level beauté isn't afraid of making a splash with brightly painted walls hung with Indian art. Even the colorful cushions add a dose of serotonin.

The menu is equally inventive and plays both sides between classic and contemporary. Start things off right with samosa chaat featuring potato-and-pea samosas laid atop curried chickpeas and streaked with tamarind sauce as well as a zesty cilantro-chili chutney. Cooked in a tandoor, chicken tikka makhani is bathed in a tomato- and caramelized-onion gravy, scented with fenugreek and ginger. The creative flair then extends to the bar, where drinks like a Mumbai Mule with rum, lime and curry leaf wet your whistle.

◼ 3512-14 Connecticut Ave. NW (bet. Ordway & Porter Sts.)
🚇 Cleveland Park
📞 (202) 244-6600 — **WEB:** www.indique.com
◼ Lunch Fri – Sun   Dinner nightly

PRICE: $$

33

THE INN AT LITTLE WASHINGTON ✿✿

American

XxxX | 🍽 🍽 🍽

MAP: N/A

Nestled in a tiny Virginia town on the edge of Shenandoah National Park—about 70 miles from the nation's capital—The Inn at Little Washington has long been the domain of Chef Patrick O'Connell and a destination in itself.

This much-lauded Southern getaway was built for celebrating special occasions. More is more when it comes to the décor of these dining rooms, as tapestries, tasseled silk lampshades, billowing fabrics, and floral patterns produce a riotous sense of opulence. Tables are elegantly set with the chef's personal collection of implements, some of which he's designed himself.

Guests choose from three tasting menus that highlight American cuisine, much of it prepared using local products pulled from the restaurant's own gardens. Tradition reigns here, as evidenced in dishes like the tin of sin: layers of American Osetra caviar with sweet crab and cucumber rillettes. Carpaccio of herb-crusted baby lamb loin pairs paper-thin slices of the meat with a spear of romaine lettuce cradling three scoops of Caesar salad dressing-flavored ice cream. Antarctic sea bass with lemon vodka sauce and Lilliputian shrimp-and-pork dumplings play up the well-balanced flavors of this regal repast.

🟦 309 Middle St. (Washington, VA)

☎ (540) 675-3800 — **WEB:** www.theinnatlittlewashington.com

🟦 Dinner Wed – Mon

PRICE: $$$$

IRON GATE ¶○

Mediterranean

✕ | 🍸 🍺 🏠 🛏

MAP: 1-C2

Tucked inside the former stables and carriageway of a historic townhouse, Iron Gate is blessed with one of the city's most charming atmospheres. The cozy dining room is complete with requisite dark wood beams, exposed brick walls, tufted leather banquettes, plus that historic cherry on top: the roaring fireplace. The trellised garden patio, heated and open most of the year, is a close second.

The kitchen features a prix-fixe dinner menu along with small plates, where the chef displays myriad riffs on Greek, Italian, and Mediterranean classics. Chilled spring pea soup is refreshing and delicate; green tomato keftedes are a vegetarian version of the traditional Greek meatballs; and crispy arancini stuffed with spinach risotto hint at spanakopita.

■ 1734 N St. NW (bet. 17th & 18th Sts.)
🚇 Dupont Circle
✆ (202) 524-5202 — WEB: www.irongaterestaurantdc.com
■ Lunch Tue – Sun Dinner nightly   PRICE: $$$

IVY CITY SMOKEHOUSE 😊

Seafood

✕ | 🍺 ♿ 🏠 🍽 🛏

MAP: 8-C1

Lucky are the eaters who make their way to this unique seafood smokehouse. Inside the warehouse-like space, a daily market and state-of-the-art smokehouse reside at street level. Above this, find a tavern-like restaurant with a large, open-air rooftop. The fish is fresh, the staff is super-friendly, and the vibe is irresistible with occasional live music.

A platter offers a broad sample of artisanal smoked goodies, like Indian candy (a sweet, salty, almost jerk-like smoked salmon); glistening, coral-pink smoked salmon; pepper-smoked salmon imbedded with crushed peppercorns; and impossibly good whitefish salad. Don't miss the chalkboard's daily specials, like tender crab cake so flaky and minimally dressed you'll think you're seaside.

■ 1356 Okie St. NE (at Fenwick St.)
✆ (202) 529-3300 — WEB: www.ivycitysmokehouse.com
■ Lunch Tue – Sun Dinner nightly   PRICE: $$

IZAKAYA SEKI 🍴

Japanese

✗

MAP: 2-C4

Set within a two-level townhouse in a residential area, Izakaya Seki delivers a simple, yet spot-on experience. With just 40 seats and a no-reservation policy, you may have to wait for your seat—either at the sushi bar on the first floor or upstairs where exposed beams and shelves lined with sake bottles make for a Kyoto-chic ambience.

The father-daughter team ventures beyond sushi and sashimi to impress diners with authentic Japanese dishes, and it is evident the chef loves what he does. Ojiya soba, lovingly prepared in Japan and dried outdoors for one year before being stirred into the dashi and topped with sweet, flavorful pork belly, is nothing if not memorable. And delicate baby octopus braised in sake and mirin is sweet, salty, and just a bit smoky.

■ 1117 V St. NW (bet. 11th & 12th Sts.)
■ U St
✆ (202) 588-5841 — **WEB:** www.sekidc.com
■ Dinner Tue – Sun

PRICE: $$

JACK ROSE DINING SALOON 🍴

American

✗✗ | 🍹 🍤

MAP: 2-A4

What can brown do for you? If you're Jack Rose, a whole lot. Brown liquor is revered here, where four walls are lined with shelves of the stuff. There are 2500 bottles and there is even a library-style, rolling wall-mounted ladder to access it. Don't worry if your head spins before you take a sip; a Scotch specialist on the premises is happy to offer advice.

Jack Rose isn't just about the bar; the kitchen delivers a hit list of gastropub-style eats. Dandelion greens pesto atop chewy fettucine is creative and flavorful; fried quail served over toast and spread with creamy sawmill gravy studded with sausage crumbles is positively delicious; and a warm mini butter cake topped with a scoop of butter-pecan ice cream is as tasty as it is adorable.

■ 2007 18th St. NW (bet. California & Vernon Sts.)
■ U St
✆ (202) 588-7388 — **WEB:** www.jackrosediningsaloon.com
■ Dinner nightly

PRICE: $$

JALEO 😊
Spanish

XX | &. &.

MAP: 3-B4

José Andrés' whimsical tapas take center stage at this outpost of Jaleo, one of three in the metro area. Sure, it has been open for over two decades, but there are no cobwebs in need of a dusting here. Creative, edgy, and irreverent, these are not your papa's tapas. Croquetas de pollo are crisped to a golden brown and stuffed with ground chicken and béchamel, then served in a resin reproduction of a Converse Chuck Taylor sneaker for a unique and amusing presentation.

DC denizens can even get a taste of El Bulli's trademark science experiment-style of cooking since Andrés and Ferran Adrià were childhood chums and Andrés spent time at El Bulli. To that end, be sure to sample Adrià's liquid olives, which make for a delicious conversation starter.

■ 480 7th St. NW (at E St.)
🚇 Gallery Pl-Chinatown
🕿 (202) 628-7949 — **WEB:** www.jaleo.com
■ Lunch & dinner daily

PRICE: $$

KAFE LEOPOLD 🍴
Austrian

XX | 🏠 🖥 &.

MAP: 7-A2

Kafe Leopold (+ Konditorei) is the exact antidote to those too-cute-for-words pastry shops. Sure, there may be 26 different desserts to tempt your sweet tooth here, but there's nothing twee about this sleek space tucked in an alley behind posh M Street. Descend the stairs and discover a lovely courtyard garden—complete with a trickling fountain—before stepping inside to a relaxed arena with eye-catching photos and a decidedly modern ambience.

Savory choices include rostbraten vom Angusrind and bratwurst, but even with their delicious homemade taste, it's the final course that is first priority. Peruse the long list of Kaffeespezialitäten, and then nibble on a slice of esterhazy (five-layer hazelnut cake), a delicious éclair, or any other can't-go-wrong treat.

■ 3315 M St. NW
🕿 (202) 965-6005 — **WEB:** www.kafeleopolds.com
■ Lunch & dinner daily

PRICE: $$

KAPNOS 🍴

Greek

XX | 🍸 ♿ 🏠 🖥 🛋 🖐

MAP: 2-B3

From the exhibition kitchen with luscious meats rotating languorously on wood-fired spits, to the chandeliers crafted of wine glasses and bottles, Kapnos is a buzzy spot that lures Capitol Hill staffers and couples on date night.

It's not just good looks; the food—mostly Greek with mezze for sharing—is just as alluring. Wood-roasted octopus tentacles are charred on the outside and tender on the inside. Follow this up with flaky phyllo pies, which when stuffed with roasted duck, are nothing less than divine. Small plates are ideal for snacking, while items like whole spit-roasted chicken or salt-baked dorado are designed for family-style dining. To chase it all down, peruse the innovative cocktail list, or opt for a glass of kegged lemonade.

■ 2201 14th St. NW (at W St.)
🚇 U St
✆ (202) 234-5000 — **WEB:** www.kapnosdc.com
■ Lunch Sat – Sun   Dinner nightly

PRICE: $$

KEREN 🍴

Ethiopian

X | 🛋

MAP: 2-A4

Go ahead and order breakfast all day long, since Keren keeps the morning meal front and center. However, before you show up expecting bacon and eggs, take a second look. Keren is a showpiece of Eritrean cuisine. This East African nation has retained the best of Italy, a once occupying force, with many Italian-influenced, pasta-centric dishes popping up on the menu. A loyal crowd alternates between watching soccer, debating Eritrean politics, and filling up on the sizable portions.

Ful, a staple breakfast dish comprised of fava beans, jalapeño, tomato, and onion, is a good place to start (there are six variations). Then opt for the "five Eritrean" dishes for a well-rounded, veg-focused combo that is so good it renders you unable to pick a favorite.

■ 1780 Florida Ave. NW (bet. 18th & U Sts.)
🚇 U St
✆ (202) 265-5764 — **WEB:** N/A
■ Lunch & dinner daily

PRICE: ⍟

KINSHIP ✿
Contemporary

XxX | ✿ ♿ ☐ 🖐

MAP: 3-B2

Kinship is much buzzed about, thanks in large part to Chef Eric Ziebold's pedigree (he cut his teeth working with Thomas Keller). Along with his wife and partner Célia Laurent, Ziebold delivers inspired cuisine to a devoted following replete with urbane gastronomes and locals.

The setting across from the convention center belies its style; the three-part space comprises a book-lined and fireplace-warmed lounge, intimate bar, and minimalist-chic dining room, all crafted by local designer, Darryl Carter.

The à la carte menu isn't just a laundry list of offerings; it's a peek inside the chef's heart and mind. While selections from the "Ingredients" and "Indulgence" categories need no explanation, "Craft" items honor tradition and "History" selections pay tribute to his sentimental favorites. Pick and choose from the different themes for a bespoke tasting menu of dishes like turmeric-braised celtuce; butter-poached Maine lobster set atop house-made caramelized brioche for a lobster French toast; and duck ballotine over celery root "tagliatelle" in a cognac sauce. For a salty thrill of a dessert, fudgy Valrhona custard cake is paired with pecan-praline ice cream and a buttery streusel.

▪ 1015 7th St. NW (bet. L St. & New York Ave.)
🚇 Mt Vernon Sq
📞 (202) 737-7700 — **WEB:** www.kinshipdc.com
▪ Dinner nightly

PRICE: $$$

KOMI ✿

Mediterranean

XX | 🍃

Climb the stairs of a historic Dupont Circle townhouse to find this diminutive restaurant with a focus on drama. The smattering of well-spaced tables and a hushed ambience fashion a very promising date night. Photos are verboten, which is no matter since you're so busy having a good time in "real" time.

The staff is relaxed, engaged, and professional. That said, they provide precious little information on how each evening's single prix-fixe will unfold—there are no menus, and diners have a minimal glimpse of what is to come next. But relinquishing control to these capable chefs (and sommelier) is the only way to go, as the results are bound to leave you feeling uplifted.

Meals begin with small bites that treat the palate to raw, cool, and cooked flavors. These have included soft brioche topped with trout roe, sliced sea scallop crudo over a lobster reduction, and sweet-savory warm Medjool dates filled with mascarpone and finished with a sprinkle of sea salt. From there, delve into a duo of wonderfully rustic house-made pastas, like ravioli filled with celery root and dressed with morels, favas, and bits of lamb's tongue. Roasted kid goat with fluffy pita conjures the best of Greece.

🔲 1509 17th St. NW (bet. P & Q Sts.)
🚇 Dupont Circle
📞 (202) 332-9200 — **WEB:** www.komirestaurant.com
🔲 Dinner Tue – Sat

PRICE: $$$$

KYIRISAN 😊

Fusion

XX | &

The Ma family's heart and soul is in this Shaw gem. It's hip, yet family-friendly, and a mix of locals, tourists, and political suits pack this energetic space.

Rabbit rillettes sandwiched between fried green tomato-turnip cakes drizzled with salted plum sriracha and sesame-soy sauce show off Chef Tim Ma's trademark blend of French-tinged Asian-flavored cooking. Sous vide duck confit is a clear winner, where moist, tender duck is sweet, smoky, and salty; balanced by caramelized Brussels sprouts; and finally offset by a tangy apple cider gastrique. One word—irresistible! All good things must come to an end, but definitely order the matcha pavlova, a matcha meringue served with black sesame-flavored whipped cream for a nutty, not-too-sweet finale.

■ 1924 8th St. NW (at Florida Ave.)
🚇 Shaw-Howard U
✆ (202) 525-2383 — **WEB:** www.kyirisandc.com
■ Dinner nightly

PRICE: $$

LA CHAUMIÈRE 🍴

French

✗ | 🖼

It may be located on a bustling Georgetown street lined with modern stores and coffee houses, but La Chaumière is as old-world as it gets—much to the delight of its loyal crowd of wealthy regulars and movers and shakers. Adorned with antique farm tools, repurposed barn wood beams, and a roaring fireplace, the dining room is both charming and cozy.

Even if the interior doesn't have you at bonjour, the food—rustic and unpretentious classics such as escargot and steak frites—will do the trick. House specials include the boudin blanc, quenelles de Brochet, and tripe stew. Of course, cassoulet is yet another house favorite. They've also managed to sneak in a few newcomers, like Maryland crab cakes, but you'll find even these cleverly Frenchified.

■ 2813 M St. NW (bet. 28th & 29th Sts.)
✆ (202) 338-1784 — **WEB:** www.lachaumieredc.com
■ Lunch Mon – Fri Dinner Mon – Sat

PRICE: $$

LAPIS 😊
Afghan

X | 🏠 | 🛋

MAP: 2-A3

Lapis-colored columns set against whitewashed walls set the tone for a restaurant that gleams like its namesake jewel. From the stunning Afghan rugs warming the floor to the sepia-toned heirloom photos on the walls, this place exudes warmth and charm, albeit in a highly stylish manner.

Husband-and-wife owners Zubair and Shamim Popal share the fragrant cuisine of their native Afghanistan. Light and fresh without the heavy-handed spicing of other regional cuisines, this food is a delicious discovery. Split pea soup may sound basic but here it is layered with flavor. And chopawn is the real deal—this trio of grilled-to-perfection lamb chops is served with sensational cardamom-scented rice and draws you in forkful after fluffy forkful.

🔲 1847 Columbia Rd. NW (at Mintwood Pl.)
📞 (202) 299-9630 — **WEB:** www.lapisdc.com
🔲 Lunch Sat – Sun   Dinner nightly

PRICE: $$

LE CHAT NOIR 🍴
French

XX | 🛋

MAP: N/A

Friendship Heights' residents are lucky indeed, as the perfect French bistro—Le Chat Noir—is nestled within their quaint neighborhood. This darling spot embodies the ideal "corner" bistro with its inviting and warm ambience and classic French cooking. It's not cutting edge, but with a panoply of French hits, who cares.

Pissaladière, typically prepared with flatbread, is literally puffed up here with a flaky pastry topped with caramelized onion, herbes de Provence, anchovies, and green olives for Mediterranean flavor. Savor the terrific broth of the bouillabaisse before tucking into the merguez aux lentilles, two thin sausage links served with green lentils set atop a salad. Savory and sweet crêpes are a mainstay of this menu, and brunch is superb.

🔲 4907 Wisconsin Ave. NW (bet. Ellicott St. & Emery Pl.)
📞 (202) 244-2044 — **WEB:** www.lechatnoirrestaurant.com
🔲 Lunch & dinner daily

PRICE: $$

LE DIPLOMATE ¶◯

French

✗✗ | ♿ ☂ ⛵   **MAP:** 1-D1

Stephen Starr takes on the nation's capital with Le Diplomate, his pitch-perfect rendition of a Rive Gauche bistro. From the shiny and large brass windows to the zinc bar and the mosaic-tiled floor, it is all très Français.

Bread lovers rejoice; there is a paean to the crusty stuff at the entrance, where ficelle-filled bags and assorted loaves and rounds are lovingly displayed. This is straightforward traditional bistro food at its best: steak tartare, croque monsieur, steak frites with sauce béarnaise, and out-of-this-world moules frites. Steamed with Pernod and served marinière-style, the mussels would be succulent enough on their own, but toss in a handful of those crispy pommes frites as well as a basket of freshly sliced baguette, and mon dieu!

▪ 1601 14th St. NW (at Q St.)
▪ U St
☎ (202) 332-3333 — **WEB:** www.lediplomatedc.com
▪ Lunch Sat – Sun   Dinner nightly   **PRICE:** $$

LITTLE SEROW ¶◯

Thai

✗   **MAP:** 1-C1

It's very black-and-white at Little Serow, a spot that's neither fancy nor fussy and a stickler for rules. For starters, there's no phone, so you can forget about reservations. The menu is fixed, and that means no changes (nope, not even for your lactose-free, gluten-free, pork-hating friend). Want more spice? Don't even try to tell them how to cook. Still interested? You'd better get in line, because the door opens promptly at 5:30 P.M.

Little Serow lures hipsters with Northern Thai cooking that isn't handcuffed to please the lowest common denominator, as well as wine pairings that perfectly complement the bold flavors. Classic minced chicken laap is ratcheted up, while the crispy fried tofu's Thai chili-enhanced sauce knocks out with a one-two punch.

▪ 1511 17th St. NW (bet. P & Q Sts.)
▪ Dupont Circle
☎ N/A — **WEB:** www.littleserow.com
▪ Dinner Tue – Sat   **PRICE:** $$

LUPO VERDE 🍴

Italian

XX | 🏠 🍽️

The neighborhood is hopping with a crowded, convivial vibe, and Lupo Verde dances to that same beat. This two-storied restaurant has an osteria feel to its downstairs level, where a Carrara marble bar and communal wood tables welcome diners. Upstairs, the dining room has a low-key but quintessential luxe Italian look.

The kitchen too boasts some unique offerings—a roasted onion stuffed with four-cheese fondue is delicious, but it's really all about the homemade pasta and spot-on affetati here. The spaghetti is gloriously thick and chewy, while the charcuterie boards are crammed with delicious imported salumi, cheeses, olives, and giardiniera. Finish with a classic affogato, in which a shot of hot espresso is poured over a dollop of creamy vanilla ice cream.

🔲 1401 T St. NW (at 14th St.)
🚇 U St
☎ (202) 827-4752 — **WEB:** www.lupoverdedc.com
🔲 Lunch Sat – Sun   Dinner nightly

PRICE: $$

MAKETTO 😀

Asian

X | 🏠 🍽️

If the hip gods of food and shopping mated, Maketto would be their love child. This unique space is equal parts style emporium and full-fledged restaurant serving sophisticated all-day dining. It may be steps from gritty H Street, but Maketto doesn't have a trace of grunge.

Taiwanese and Cambodian recipes influence the kitchen's appetizing, yet unexpected, Asian cuisine. Coconut milk-scallop crudo is at once razor-thin and ebulliently flavorful; a Taiwanese fried oyster omelette packs an eggy, briny punch; and grilled fish with coconut nam prik will elicit envy from your neighboring tables. If you have friends in tow, tuck in to the bountiful bao platter and its host of fillers, including those salty-sweet, perfectly marinated slices of rib eye.

🔲 1351 H St. NE (bet. Linden Ct. & 14th St.)
☎ (202) 838-9972 — **WEB:** www.maketto1351.com
🔲 Lunch daily   Dinner Mon – Sat

PRICE: $$

MAKOTO ⁑🍽

Japanese

❌❌

Makoto is a testament to the love between a father and son. The chef, who assumed the top spot when his father passed some years ago, is warm and generous with stories of his father's passion and sacrifice. This place isn't about trend and there is a palpable sense of honoring tradition, so make a reservation, dress up, and expect to shed your shoes at the door.

You won't find à la carte sushi here, but you will be rewarded with a litany of skillfully prepared dishes. Seared Turkish royal sea bass with grilled asparagus and sugar snap peas along with a roasted red pepper sauce displays harmonious balance. Then, pan-seared sea urchin with crispy rice cake, burnt nori, and kinome leaf, sprinkled with green seaweed is named a signature for good reason.

▪ 4822 MacArthur Blvd. NW (bet. Reservoir Rd. & W St.)
✆ (202) 298-6866 — **WEB:** www.makotorestaurantdc.com
▪ Dinner Tue – Thu   **PRICE: $$$**

MANDU ⁑🍽

Korean

❌ | 🏠 🍴

MAP: 2-A4

You don't come to Mandu with your high-maintenance fashionista friend. But, if you're seeking the real deal—authentic and delicious Korean food without a lot of fuss—it is just the place. Everything is made with love at this family-owned original, and the portions are generous (especially at brunch, which is also light on the wallet).

Stick to the stews—dak jjim or soon doobu, yokge jang, and mandu guk—before moving up to the more hearty galbi or bulgogi. Kimchi jjigae has a heady perfume of garlic, chilies, and onions that announces its presence right after leaving the semi-open kitchen. And the kimchi bokum bap, heaped into a deep stone bowl, has a sweet-spicy sauce and is flavored with just the right amount of gochujang to add color and extra oomph.

▪ 1805 18th St. NW (bet. S & Swann Sts.)
🚇 Dupont Circle
✆ (202) 588-1540 — **WEB:** www.mandudc.com
▪ Lunch & dinner daily   **PRICE: $$**

MARCEL'S ¶○

French

XxX | 88 ⅊ ⊡ ⬦

Marcel's may lure a who's who crowd to its elegantly understated dining room, but there's nothing uppity about the amiable and genuine staff, who expertly walk the tightrope between attentive and fussy. Patrons come to linger over French-influenced meals enjoyed over multiple courses.

Pan-seared foie gras atop duck confit paired with eau de vie-soaked cherries, or grilled quail over a warm artichoke salad are certainly French inspired. Curried butternut squash soup with apple, black sesame, and toasted cashew or enoki mushroom-topped halibut over parsnip purée speak to an entirely different influence. The almond financier with sunflower ice cream might be overdressed with too many flourishes, but with its buttery goodness, nobody is complaining.

▪ 2401 Pennsylvania Ave. NW (bet. 24th & 25th Sts.)
▪ Foggy Bottom-GWU
℘ (202) 296-1166 — **WEB:** www.marcelsdc.com
▪ Lunch Sun Dinner nightly   **PRICE: $$$$**

MINTWOOD PLACE ¶○

American

XX | 🍸 🍄 ⬦

Take a chic Parisian and a ten gallon-hat-wearing cowboy and blend for an improbable but oh-so-happy mix and you have Mintwood Place. This Western saloon-style space does Adams Morgan proud with its fun-loving, quirky feel defined by wood paneling, wrought-iron accents, and a rooster- and wagon wheel-enhanced décor.

Don't worry though, as this melting pot of American and French cooking is anything but hokey. Snack on deviled eggs and pickled rhubarb before digging into escargot hushpuppies, a glorious Franco-American meeting of the minds. Starters like goat cheese and beet mountain pie or duck pâté entice with French finesse, while entrées like shrimp and grits or smoked pork ribs are stick-to-your-ribs, Southern-style good. Key lime pie is perfection.

▪ 1813 Colombia Rd. NW (bet. Biltmore St. & Mintwood Pl.)
℘ (202) 234-6732 — **WEB:** www.mintwoodplace.com
▪ Lunch Sat – Sun Dinner Tue – Sun   **PRICE: $$$**

MASERIA ✿

Italian

XX | 🍸 🍹 ♿ 🏠

MAP: 8-A2

With its chic and seamless blend of indoor and outdoor space, Masseria is a clear departure from its rough-and-tumble neighborhood. The classic former warehouse—complete with the requisite exposed ducts, concrete floors, and brick walls—has been glammed up with a stainless steel exhibition kitchen, chrome and leather furnishings, pendant lights suspended from nautical rope, and an impressive glass-encased wine cellar.

It's all very relaxed, albeit in a well-dressed way, and the feel-good vibe extends to the staff, who clearly like working here as much as diners enjoy lingering over the multi-course meals.

The chef's Puglian heritage comes through in the menu, which features three to five courses, along with a nightly tasting menu. The kitchen hits all the right notes balancing trendy and serious. Begin with a cigar box filled with focaccia so sinfully delicious, you'll be tempted to scarf it all down—but don't. You'll want to save room for the spicy fish stew, a thing of beauty practically brimming with tripe and lobster, or house-made maccheroni with a thick and gamey goat ragù. Even dessert strays far from the pack, showcasing beet ice cream instead of the classic tiramisu.

■ 1340 4th St. NE (bet. Neal Pl. & Penn St.)
🚇 NoMa-Gallaudet U
☏ (202) 608-1330 — **WEB:** www.masseria-dc.com
■ Dinner Tue – Sat

PRICE: $$$

MÉTIER ⭐

Contemporary

✕✕✕ | 🕸 🦽 ⟷ 🧼

Find this mature, splurge-worthy tasting room beneath its slightly casual sister-spot, Kinship. They may share a kitchen and chef/owner, but these are two distinct restaurants.

Guests enter Métier via an elevator, which then leads to a second, more sultry lounge. With a fireplace and shelves lined with cookbooks, this is a lovely stop for cocktails and nibbles. One part living room and two parts art gallery, the sleek arena is a spare collection of cloth-robed tables and white walls with paintings here and there. This is one of those few remaining places where jackets are required, so gentlemen, don't forget to don them!

The name, Métier, is defined as an area of expertise, and that proves true in an ambitious menu reflective of Chef Eric Ziebold's experience. A meal's luxe opening may reveal butter-braised La Ratte potatoes set over lemony crème fraîche with bonito shavings and Osetra caviar. Love for meat is clear in the tableside presentation of lamb loin, served with the hay in which it was smoked, laid over goat cheese, and finished with a sauce of tomatoes, white wine, and oregano. For dessert, a deconstructed New England apple pie is the perfect blend of sweet and salty flavors.

🔲 1015 7th St. NW (bet. L St. & New York Ave.)
🚇 Mt Vernon Sq
📞 (202) 737-7500 — **WEB:** www.metierdc.com
🔲 Dinner Tue – Sat

PRICE: $$$$

MINIBAR ✿✿

Contemporary

XX | 🦞 🍸 ♿ 🍽 🤝

At the base of an unremarkable building, find two frosted doors marking the entrance to minibar—a restaurant that extends well beyond its diminutive name. The stylish entry lounge is an idyllic stop for a glass of bubbly before heading into the elegant dining room. Here, guests are situated at six seats per dining counter, all set around Chef José Andrés' stainless steel workspace that literally makes his world a stage.

As expected, this kitchen is superbly orchestrated, highlighting foams, flowers, intricate compositions, and extreme dexterity—with tweezers, of course. Plates are crafted from pottery, aloe vera, or bamboo leaves, ensuring that creativity is as much in the eye as on the palate. The repast may begin with a unique cocktail, like Barr Hill vodka, made from honey, served in a beeswax cup, and drizzled with more honey from the same Vermont bees. Playful course after course reminds one that a snail is not just a snail here, but a dome of Ibérico ham gel, formed like that mollusk, served with rabbit jus and escargot roe. A final dessert course arrives as a porcelain T-rex bearing Key lime bonbons and trompe l'oeil "peanuts" that are nutty confections filled with Bourbon gel.

■ 855 E St. NW (at 9th St.)
🚇 Gallery Pl-Chinatown
📞 (202) 393-0812 — **WEB:** www.minibarbyjoseandres.com
■ Dinner Tue – Sat

PRICE: $$$$

MIRABELLE ☂🍴

French

XX | 🍸 ♿ ⛱ 💠 🎿

MAP: 1-C3

From its walnut-framed tufted leather walls and Carrara marble floors to the smoky mirrors and captivating double-spouted absinthe fountain, this no-expense-spared stunner just blocks from the White House does wonders for French-American relations. And thanks to heavy-hitters Frank Ruta and Aggie Chin, the classic brasserie food is as polished as the scene.

Sip a cocktail or glass of wine from the well-chosen list before diving in to crowd-pleasing dishes such as oven-roasted poussin, enhanced with a deliciously rich crayfish-mushroom cream sauce. Beef tartare, in all of its glistening ruby glory, is textbook perfect. Then there's dessert—mais oui! Tarte Tatin, yuzu sesame mille crêpe, or butterscotch crémeux practically deserve to be eaten first.

🔲 900 16th St. NW (at I St.)
🔲 Farragut West
✆ (202) 506-3833 — **WEB:** www.mirabelledc.com
🔲 Lunch Mon – Fri   Dinner Mon – Sat

PRICE: $$$

MOMOFUKU CCDC 🍴

Asian

XX | ♿ 💠

MAP: 3-A2

David Chang has come a long way since his tiny game-changing original in New York City's East Village. This impressive DC outpost is bright and shiny with multiple levels, lots of glass, and textbook-contemporary décor (think backless blonde wood stools).

Chang's signature street-style food is what put him on the map, and that's exactly what you'll find here. Those buzzed-about buns (let's face it, that's what you came for) are the stuff that pilgrimages are made of: pillowy soft, stuffed with meat or shrimp and slathered with tangy sauces. Rice cakes are yet another favored dish, while braised fried chicken is oh-so-good. Located just off the main dining room, the takeout Milk Bar carries desserts like the famed crack pie.

🔲 1090 I St. NW (at New York Ave.)
🔲 McPherson Square
✆ (202) 602-1832 — **WEB:** www.ccdc.momofuku.com
🔲 Lunch & dinner daily

PRICE: $$

NAZCA MOCHICA 🍴⟵

Peruvian

✗✗ | 🍸 🏠 🛋️

In a Peruvian version of upstairs-downstairs, this two-in-one restaurant comprises a cebiche and pisco bar downstairs with more traditional dining and a sleeker style upstairs. Luckily, the fantastic cebiches are served both up and down. Causitas are the ultimate spud lover's comfort food and feature four towers of baked whipped potatoes topped with different flavors: caramelized fatty pork belly and onions; chicken salad dressed in mild aji amarillo; tuna cebiche with cilantro shoots; and slivered roasted piquillo peppers.

Kobe short ribs are glazed with a terrific, mildly spicy aji panca-honey, accompanied by yuca, potatoes, and choclo in a creamy huancaina sauce. In the end, sugar-dusted alfajores filled with dulce de leche round out the meal.

◾ 1633 P St. NW (bet. 17th & 16th Sts.)
🏛️ Dupont Circle
☎ (202) 733-3170 — **WEB:** www.nazcamochica.com
◾ Lunch daily   Dinner Tue – Sun

PRICE: $$

OBELISK 🍴⟵

Italian

✗

MAP: 1-B1

Obelisk attracts a surprisingly young, casual crowd for a spot that has been serving a fixed five-course menu five nights a week since 1987—a fact that's likely due to the restaurant's warm, neighborhood feel, even if the townhome it's set in could use a revamp.

The light and seasonal Italian cooking begins with a bang as an assortment of fantastic antipasti are quickly ushered to the table: creamy burrata; a sardine served over a tasty Prosecco-braised onion salad; crunchy puntarelle salad with a creamy anchovy dressing; and a thin slice of porchetta with a crisp shell and rich, flavorful meaty center, to name a few. The second and third courses are overshadowed by the first, but the full experience is worth the two to three hours to enjoy.

◾ 2029 P St. NW (bet. 20th & 21st Sts.)
🏛️ Dupont Circle
☎ (202) 872-1180 — **WEB:** www.obeliskdc.com
◾ Dinner Tue – Sat

PRICE: $$$

OLD GLORY BARBECUE ¶○

Barbecue

XX | 🍺 🏕

Though it skews more hipster than provincial, Old Glory Barbecue remains unpretentious all the same. Inside, it's all weathered wooden booths, worn stools, a bar studded with 1901 silver dollars, and rustic Americana décor, while upstairs is a popular patio that's heated during colder months.

Leave the white shirt at home since this succulent stuff will end up everywhere. Old Glory doesn't pick sides, so most regional styles are celebrated here with equal love and distinction. Stacked atop a soft potato roll, pulled pork is juicy and glistening with a tart and spicy sauce, while hearty beef ribs are slow-cooked for eight hours and fall-off-the-bone tender with a sweet and smoky flavor that will have you gnawing like a dog on the bone.

■ 3139 M St. NW (bet. Wisconsin Ave. & 31st St.)
✆ (202) 337-3406 — **WEB:** www.oldglorybbq.com
■ Lunch & dinner daily

PRICE: $$

OSTERIA MORINI ¶○

Italian

XX | ♿ 🏕 🍷

Yards Park is shaking things up along the Anacostia River, and Osteria Morini is among the high-profile restaurants headlining the riverfront rags-to-riches development. Thanks to its giant windows, abundant natural light, and open kitchen, this sleek and airy space truly shines.

One of several spinoffs of Michael White's original in New York's SoHo, the menu manages to be both impressive and familiar. Get the much-touted burger, which is celebrated at lunch and is also a nod to DC's less adventurous palates. Other items may also include wood-grilled meats, homemade pasta, and polpettine in brodo. Most impressive, however, is the generous bowl of conchiglie topped with pecorino fonduta, a culinary delight that screams "dig in" like nothing else.

■ 301 Water St. SE (bet. 3rd & 4th Sts.)
🚇 Navy Yard-Ballpark
✆ (202) 484-0660 — **WEB:** www.osteriamorini.com
■ Lunch & dinner daily

PRICE: $$$

OTTOMAN TAVERNA 😋

Turkish

XX | 🍺 ♿ 🏠 📷 🛋️   **MAP:** 3-C2

This place is fit for a king. The interior is drop-dead gorgeous with a can't-stop-staring beauty. From its honeycomb patterns on the walls and that large mural of the Hagia Sophia, to its whitewashed walls with glimmering deep-blue pendants, this restaurant brings a little bit of Istanbul to the Mt. Vernon Triangle.

Sip a cool apple-rose tea while perusing the menu of Turkish cuisine infused with a modern bent. Kirmizi mercimek corbasi is a refreshing red lentil soup that starts things off right. Then dive in to thinly sliced and delicious lamb and beef kebabs. But it's the moussaka, with its supple eggplant and potato slices and cinnamon-scented lamb, that must not be skipped. Freshly baked baklava or Noah's pudding end the meal on a syrupy note.

■ 425 I St. NW (bet. 4th & 5th Sts.)
🏙 Gallery Pl-Chinatown
📞 (202) 847-0395 — **WEB:** www.ottomantaverna.com
■ Lunch & dinner daily   **PRICE: $$**

THE OVAL ROOM 🍴

Contemporary

XxX | ♿ 🏠 📷 🖐️   **MAP:** 1-C4

The Oval Room has been the restaurant of choice for a particular brand of Beltway insider for over two decades, but like any doyenne worth her salt, this place underwent a recent nip and tuck to keep everything fresh. The dining room oozes sophistication with its plush carpeting and museum-style artwork. This elegance also extends outdoors to the chic sidewalk.

The food echoes the sophisticated environs with well-prepared classics, such as chicken liver mousse and crisp-skinned Amish roast chicken with Brussels sprouts, wild mushrooms, sweet peas, favas, and shaved truffle. Other entrées, such as shrimp and coconut grits with shellfish butter, or even molasses-glazed pork belly with cornbread purée show off a creative and Southern-inspired flair.

■ 800 Connecticut Ave. NW (bet. 16th & 17th Sts.)
🏙 Farragut West
📞 (202) 463-8700 — **WEB:** www.ovalroom.com
■ Lunch Mon – Fri   Dinner Mon – Sat   **PRICE: $$$**

OYAMEL 😊

Mexican

XX | 🔲 🛋

Oyamel dishes out all the flavor of Mexico in a funky, festive space that delivers a quick hit of happiness. Snag a seat at the wraparound bar and guzzle thirst-quenching drinks while snacking on a parade of small plates, and you'll find that the rumors are true: José Andrés knows his stuff.

The kitchen's dedication to techniques and ingredients is clear, though the authentic south-of-the-border food far outshines the mediocre tacos. Huevos enfrijolados are a must order, crispy chilaquiles are spot on, and gorditas topped with Hudson Valley duck confit are nothing like their disagreeable Taco Bell cousins. The charred salsa is good enough to drink, with the perfect balance of acidity and flavor, and Andrés' take on tres leches offers a decadently sweet finish.

🔳 401 7th St. NW (bet. D & E Sts.)
🚇 Archives
📞 (202) 628-1005 — WEB: www.oyamel.com
🔳 Lunch & dinner daily

PRICE: $$

THE PARTISAN 🍴

Gastropub

XX | 🍺 ♿ 🛋

It shares space with sib Red Apron, a butcher shop and gourmet boutique, but The Partisan wins votes for its gastropub grub and hip feel. It is tall, dark, and handsome: picture industrial-height ceilings with exposed air ducts and a moody-broody color scheme.

Beer is big here, with 17 on draft arranged by flavor profile (tart/funky and fruit/spice are just two). At lunch, pick a meat (turkey breast, porchetta, or beef döner), then take your tigelle or flatbread, and "smoosh" it all together. At night, the menu steers offbeat and may include crawfish hushpuppies, beer-brined rotisserie duck, or smoked pork with mescal-baked beans. Charcuterie is also creative unveiling absinthe-lime rillettes, negroni-inspired Campari-rosemary salami, and curried pork pâté.

🔳 709 D St. NW (bet. 7th & 8th Sts.)
🚇 Archives
📞 (202) 524-5322 — WEB: www.thepartisandc.com
🔳 Lunch & dinner daily

PRICE: $$

PEARL DIVE OYSTER PALACE 😊

Southern

XX | 🍴 🛋 **MAP:** 1-D1

With its slightly nautical ambience and casual pub vibe, this spot makes an ideal clubhouse for play-hard types. And while places that look this good usually don't have the menu to match, Pearl Dive's kitchen gives the dining room a run for its money.

The lineup is true-blue American food with a Southern slant, spotlighting starters like crunchy crawfish fritters, regional gumbos, and entrées like Tchoupitoulas—oyster confit with blue crab, Tasso ham, as well as roasted corn. And then there are the incredible oysters, which are part of the Oyster Recovery Project (meaning you can feel good while you slurp them up with abandon). On your way out, make like the smug, in-the-know patrons and order the Brazos River-bottom pecan pie to go.

🟦 1612 14th St. NW (bet. Q & Corcoran Sts.)
🟦 U St
✆ (202) 319-1612 — **WEB:** www.pearldivedc.com
🟦 Lunch Fri – Sun   Dinner nightly   **PRICE: $$**

PINEA 🍴

Mediterranean

XX | ♿ 🍽 🛋 🛋 🍽 **MAP:** 1-D4

Tucked inside the swanky W Hotel, Pinea's Beaux-Arts dining room boasts stunning murals by Baltimore artist, Gaia. It's the kind of jaw-dropping space that makes for a tough act to follow, but Chef Barry Koslow exceeds expectation with a Mediterranean-inspired menu of mouthwatering antipasti, ethereal homemade pastas, and striking seafood creations.

Kick things off with a remarkably light saffron linguine, tossed with succulent crab, red chili, and basil-kissed breadcrumbs. Then move on to a thick tranche of pearly white pan-seared striped bass, served with olive oil-crushed potatoes, braised escarole and preserved lemon. After dinner, head down to the speakeasy-like Root Cellar Whiskey Bar for cozy conversation and a serious cocktail.

🟦 515 15th St. NW (at F St.)
✆ (202) 661-2400 — **WEB:** www.pineadc.com
🟦 Lunch & dinner daily   **PRICE: $$$**

PINEAPPLE AND PEARLS ⁑ ⁑

Contemporary

XX | 🦀 🍸 & 🤲

MAP: 4-C2

What makes this "pearl" such a memorable dining experience is that the cooking is ambitious yet whimsical, and completely devoid of formality or fuss. Whether the bartender or Chef Aaron Silverman himself serves you, no one in this kitchen seems self-important. Your continued enjoyment is paramount—an honorable feat considering that you are in for a meal that occupies most of your night. The place may be packed, but the ambience is pleasant and very comfortable. Know that the prix fixe includes wine pairings, but guests seated at the bar may choose to order drinks à la carte instead. No matter where you land, dishes spark interest and service remains at its highest level.

Begin your feast with a fennel bonbon set in demi-spheres of chocolate, served in an absinthe spoon, and set over a cocktail of sunchoke and absinthe. Garnished with celery leaves and fennel fronds, it's no wonder this composition is a surefire. Then a shallow bowl bearing cubes of smoked sturgeon stacked with beets, apple, leeks, and finished with lemon zest, chervil, and smoked sturgeon consommé is as beautiful as it is delicious.

Desserts never fail to surprise, with delicacies like the wonderful Okinawan potato ice cream.

■ 715 8th St. SE (bet. G & I Sts.)
🚇 Eastern Market
✆ (202) 595-7375 — **WEB:** www.pineappleandpearls.com
■ Dinner Tue – Fri

PRICE: $$$$

PLUME ✿

European

XxxX | 🕸 ♿ 🍽 🤚

Gentlemen don a jacket and ladies grab those pearls because dinner at this dining room of The Jefferson Hotel is a very elegant affair. Walk past marble pillars, check-in at Plume's reception desk, and expect to be cordially escorted to your table in this sequestered lair.

Gilded and sparkling, the dining room's opulence pays homage to America's colonial grandeur with plush silk wallpaper depicting the grounds of Thomas Jefferson's Monticello. Large tables spread over checkerboard-tiled floors are laid with sumptuously starched linens, polished silver, and heavy crystal; while bright flowers pop against the room's aubergine-hued accents. A roaring fireplace is a cozy wintertime bonus.

This modern menu applies classic European technique to a bevy of local ingredients that are inspired by the seasons. The prix-fixe unveils an evening of gastronomic opportunity. Regulars know to commence with the Chesapeake Bay Blue Crab tea. This tableside preparation is a succulent distillation poured over myriad garnishes. King salmon slow-poached in hot beeswax is another showstopper; and Pavlova with crystallized violets and strained yogurt proves this kitchen is solid from start to finish.

🟦 1200 16th St. NW (at M St.)
🚇 Farragut North
📞 (202) 448-2300 — **WEB:** www.plumedc.com
🟦 Dinner Tue – Sat

PRICE: $$$$

PROOF 🍴

American

✗✗ | 🎴 ♿ 🍄

It may be said that the proof is in the pudding, but this particular restaurant proves its mettle with wine. Inside, contemporary pendant lights, dark wood floors, and walls showcasing bottles of, yes, wine, have a chic and modern effect. The liquid is more than artwork, though, and oenophiles and newbies alike will find satisfying sips.

Proof's food reflects an international point of view—envision flaky and glistening flatbread topped with chickpeas, red onion, green olives, pickled radish, and a silky, smoked eggplant emulsion; or spicy chicken and pork meatballs paired with ricotta ravioli. If you manage to leave room for dessert, consider forgoing something sweet and instead sink your teeth into a selection from the comprehensive cheese list.

◼ 775 G St. NW (at 8th St.)
🚇 Gallery Pl-Chinatown
☏ (202) 737-7663 — **WEB:** www.proofdc.com
◼ Lunch Tue – Fri   Dinner nightly

PRICE: $$

PURPLE PATCH 🍴

Filipino

✗✗ | 🛋

How do you pay tribute to the classics while simultaneously bumping them up ever so much? Just ask the Purple Patch. This restaurant delivers note-perfect Filipino food with just the right amount of playfulness. Case in point? The adobo-radicchio wraps, which take the familiar flavors of chicken in adobo, top it with pickled papaya, then surround it with the crunch of radicchio. Pork sinigang is considered a typical (read staple) dish, but is truly worthy of exaltation. Here, tender chunks of pork are bathed in a lemon broth that is so generously sized it seems indecent, and with potatoes, vegetables, and fluffy jasmine rice, it's plain sinful.

Even dessert is a thing of wonder. Purple yam ice cream? Who knew a tuber could be this magically delicious?

◼ 3155 Mt. Pleasant St. NW (bet. Keyton St. & Kilbourne Pl.)
🚇 Columbia Heights
☏ (202) 299-0022 — **WEB:** www.purplepatchdc.com
◼ Lunch Sat – Sun   Dinner nightly

PRICE: ⊜

RAPPAHANNOCK OYSTER BAR ⚔️〇

Seafood

✗ | 🍹 ♿ ⛱

MAP: 8-A2

Set inside the buzzing Union Market, Rappahannock Oyster Bar is oh-so-much more than a popular bivalve joint. The feel-good revival story behind it will make you feel more philanthropist than hungry diner, and the ambience is everything you'd expect and then some: counter space, communal seating, a sprinkling of outdoor tables, and an open-air vibe.

While the spotlight here is on the raw bar (order the sampler, a veritable love letter to the Virginia waters), the cooked dishes give those half-shells a run for their money. Clam chowder is thick, creamy, and full of briny meat, and though the steamed shrimp dish sounds simple, these spicy shell-on specimens, served with a hunk of bread, sautéed onions, and peppers are a messy but delicious affair.

◼ 1309 5th St. NE (in Union Market)
🚇 NoMa-Gallaudet U
✆ (202) 544-4702 — **WEB:** www.rroysters.com
◼ Lunch & dinner Tue – Sun

PRICE: $$

RASIKA ⚔️〇

Indian

✗✗ | 🖥 🤚

MAP: 3-B4

This ever-popular hot spot lures all types with its kitsch-free Indian cuisine and the kind of lively, low-key ambience that's as perfectly suited for a casual night out with friends as it is a formal dinner with colleagues or festive celebration.

It's difficult to live up to the hype, but Rasika turns out several winning dishes. Palak chaat's crispy spinach leaves tossed with raita, sweet tamarind and date chutneys bursts with flavor, and the tender, yet crunchy okra is a perfect marriage of spicy and sour. Match these with expertly prepared, house-made paneer skewered with peppers and onions and accompanied by tangy green chutney.

For those who can't get a table, Rasika has a second, less-trafficked location in the West End with a similar menu.

◼ 633 D St. NW (bet. 6th & 7th Sts.)
✆ (202) 637-1222 — **WEB:** www.rasikarestaurant.com
◼ Lunch Mon – Fri   Dinner Mon – Sat

PRICE: $$$

THE RED HEN 🐾

American

✗

MAP: 2-D4

You can't miss this place—there's a giant red hen painted on the façade of the century-old building—but if you're a Bloomingdale resident, you're likely a regular already. The look is farmhouse funky complete with reclaimed timber, exposed brick, and a wood-burning oven in the kitchen, but don't let the country-cute appeal fool you: there's a CIA-trained chef manning the stove. It's largely American with an Italian accent, plus a few offbeat ingredients (shichimi togarashi and za'atar) thrown in for good measure.

Pasta is a sure thing, and the crowd favorite, mezze rigatoni with fennel sausage ragù, is sealing testimony that simple isn't boring. Caramelized scallops atop creamy polenta are delicious, but save room for the just-sweet-enough maple custard.

▪ 1822 1st St. NW (at Seaton Pl.)
✆ (202) 525-3021 — **WEB:** www.theredhendc.com
▪ Dinner nightly

PRICE: $$

RIS 🍴

American

✗✗ | ♿ 🏠 🛋

MAP: 1-A3

Ris Lacoste helms the stove at this terrific neighborhood spot, a draw for diners in the company of family, business associates, and lovers alike. The sprawling, light-filled dining room is dressed in earth tones and filled with intimate corners for an air of seductive sophistication. And the menu, with its ramped-up take on the tried-and-true, toes the line between familiar and surprising.

Loaded with butter and olive oil and jazzed up with red pepper flakes, linguine with clams is briny and delicious, and chicken Milanese has just the right amount of breading beneath its zippy tomato topping. Even the crown of cauliflower is interesting and complex, thanks to an ensemble of roasted vegetables slicked with mustard cream and an army of flavors.

▪ 2275 L St. NW (at 23rd St.)
🚇 Foggy Bottom-GWU
✆ (202) 730-2500 — **WEB:** www.risdc.com
▪ Lunch Sun – Fri   Dinner nightly

PRICE: $$

ROSE'S LUXURY ✿

Contemporary

XX | 🍸 ⛩ 🏺

MAP: 4-C2

Despite its prime Capitol Hill location, there's nothing buttoned up about Rose's Luxury. This local fave's food and mood practically sings of funkier digs.

Tucked inside a row house, the cozy-yet-contemporary space is industrial-chic to a tee with bare plywood banquettes, concrete accents, and strings of lights. The youthful-cum-playful atmosphere is bolstered by a hipster-heavy crowd, who queue up early or outsource a placeholder in line for this no-reservations spot.

Innovative yet approachable, the food bobs and weaves with absolute precision. Its melting pot of flavors is dizzying at times, and every dish is far from forgettable. Choose from cool or warm small plates: charred carrots tempered by tart house-made yogurt with harissa for extra pizzazz; crispy, complex jerk spice-marinated fried pig's ears; or an intensely elaborate salad of pork sausage, habanero, peanuts, and lychee. Pasta is turned on its head with unorthodox blends like a tomato-rich penne alla vodka pepped up with Thai basil. And while several family-style dishes are also on offer, the small plates are far more intriguing. To end the meal on a sweet note, dig in to the befuddling—yet delicious—Fernet and cola tiramisu.

🟦 717 8th St. SE (bet. G & I Sts.)
🚇 Eastern Market
📞 (202) 580-8889 — **WEB:** www.rosesluxury.com
🟦 Dinner Mon – Sat

PRICE: $$

ROYAL 🐶
Latin American

✗✗ | 🍸 🍳
MAP: 2-D4

They may not be regal, but there's a family behind Royal. The owner, along with his parents and sister, have a hand in this all-day dining spot designed for residents who want to eat well without breaking the bank. Budgets aside, Royal doesn't scrimp on style or flavor either. Tin-ceilings and other original touches were retained and the vibe is welcoming, yet casual (no reservations or hostess).

Golden-brown empanadas with paper-thin exteriors are stuffed with juicy pork for a taste of mama's Colombian kitchen and the aji is so good, you can't get enough of it. Chicken and sprouts sure sounds basic, but given the tender grilled drumsticks accompanied by roasted Brussels sprouts and charred scallions with a chimi-style white sauce, it's anything but.

🔲 501 Florida Ave. NW (at 5th St.)
🚇 Shaw-Howard U
📞 (202) 332-7777 — **WEB:** www.theroyaldc.com
🔲 Lunch & dinner daily
PRICE: $$

SAKURAMEN 🍴○
Japanese

✗
MAP: 2-A3

Sometimes all you really want is a delicious meal in a comfortable setting. No fuss, no hipper-than-thou patrons, just good food. Sakuramen, in the basement of a row house in Adams Morgan, is on hand to soothe your soul with its wide variety of that steaming bowl of love—ramen.

In fact, it's all about these toothsome noodles here. Goji ramen is a traditional shoyu ramen, while chosun shows off a Korean influence with Angus bulgogi and kimchi. Gyoza and steamed buns are available for good measure. Sakuramen is naturally the house special and the kitchen changes things up with a vegetable broth made from mushrooms and seaweed. Braised bamboo shoots, portobello caps, and other vegetables bob amid the curly noodles for a perfectly satisfying meal.

🔲 2441 18th St. NW (bet. Belmont & Columbia Rds.)
📞 (202) 656-5285 — **WEB:** www.sakuramen.info
🔲 Lunch Fri – Sun   Dinner Tue – Sun
PRICE: 🍝

1789 🍴🍷

American

XX | 🕸 💠 🤚   **MAP:** 7-A2

Housed on a quaint street, 1789 is classic Georgetown—think wooden beams, antiques, and fireplaces all nestled inside a historic, Federal period townhouse. The restaurant's six dining rooms, each with their own layout and décor, are spread across three floors and packed with a global, multi-generational crowd.

The mood here is definitely special occasion, and the menu bows to that by sticking with what works: straightforward, seasonal, and carefully curated American fare. Maryland crab fondue set over silky mashed potatoes and topped with uni is winningly simple; while wonderfully moist duck breast is dressed up with a foie gras truffle for a tasty garnish. Coconut milk cream with passion fruit crèmeux is that ideal yin and yang of sweet and tart.

🔲 1226 36th St. NW (at Prospect St.)
📞 (202) 965-1789 — **WEB:** www.1789restaurant.com
🔲 Dinner nightly   **PRICE: $$$$**

SFOGLINA 😊

Italian

XX | 👤 🚻 🍸   **MAP:** 6-C1

This focused, consistent, and lovely trattoria serves the kind of Italian cooking that everyone wants to return to again and again. The slender room is instantly welcoming with its working pasta station and a whimsical portrait of Sophia Loren. The name (Italian for "pasta master") sets a very high bar but lives up to its moniker with a notable variety of hearty and elegant preparations listed as "classical" and "seasonal." Highlights have included short, twin tubes of fresh casarecce dressed Amalfi-style with tender octopus, lobster, and a luscious sauce of savory stock, tomatoes, and paprika, finished with chives.

End with a soft swirl of vanilla bean-flecked sweet cream gelato and strawberry sorbetto, garnished with macerated berries.

🔲 4445 Connecticut Ave. NW (at Yuma St.)
🚇 Van Ness-UDC
📞 (202) 450-1312 — **WEB:** www.sfoglinadc.com
🔲 Lunch Tue – Sun   Dinner nightly   **PRICE: $$**

THE SMITH ⑪〇

Gastropub

XX | 🍹 ♿ 🛋 🍴

MAP: 3-A3

The Smith may be fresh on the scene, but it boasts four locations in New York. This European brasserie is decorated with basic wood furnishings, foxed mirror panels, and white-tiled walls. The warmly lit zinc bar showcases sparkling-wine cocktails, punch, and drink specials like Moscow mules with house-made ginger beer. A tall communal table is ideal for gathering with friends.

The crowd-pleasing carte features comfort food, like chicken pot pie, shellfish platters, and mussels steamed in chardonnay. Lunchtime faves unveil rigatoni with wilted pea shoots and tomatoes dressed in parsley-almond pesto, while nightly specials culminate in a Saturday paella. Come on your special day for a slice of chocolate birthday cake, which is always on the menu.

◾ 901 F St. NW (at 9th St.)
🏙 Gallery Pl-Chinatown
✆ (202) 868-4900 — **WEB:** www.thesmithrestaurant.com
◾ Lunch & dinner daily
PRICE: $$

SOI 38 ⑪〇

Thai

XX | ⛱

MAP: 1-A3

Sidewalk seating is plentiful, but step inside Soi 38 and you'll discover a delightfully modern and elegant dining room. Black walls are emblazoned with gold-painted images, making a dramatic first impression. While the look is upscale, the menu celebrates the street foods of Thailand, offering a blend of influences from the owners' native Bangkok and the chef's Northern Thai heritage.

Begin with khao soi, hailing from Chiang Mai and filled to the brim with a turmeric-yellow, dried chili, and coconut milk curry bursting with chicken and noodles. Kua kling is a ground pork curry served with cucumber and green beans over rice; while seua rong hai is that holy grail of expertly grilled flank steak coupled with a spicy and crunchy green papaya salad.

◾ 2101 L St. NW (entrance on 21st St.)
🏙 Farragut North
✆ (202) 558-9215 — **WEB:** www.soi38dc.com
◾ Lunch & dinner daily
PRICE: $$

SONOMA ♍⚮

Contemporary

✗✗ | ⚬ ♿ 🏠 💄 🔥   **MAP:** 4-A1

This popular wine bar is just the spot to unwind after a long day on the Hill. Exposed brick walls and a polished wood-backed banquette are at once laid-back and luxe, while the sidewalk out front offers a breath of fresh air. Despite its name, Sonoma features an extensive global wine list, and by-the-glass offerings are numerous. Take a sip around the world with a flight like The Yellow Brick Road, which spotlights a trio of sauvignon blancs from Bordeaux, New Zealand, and Napa.

The impressive list of house-crafted charcuterie includes pork rillettes, pâté de campagne, gravlax, and chicken liver mousse. However, heartier appetites will meet their match with burgers, pizzas, and pasta, including gnocchi with an eggplant ragù akin to ratatouille.

◼ 223 Pennsylvania Ave. SE (bet. Independence Ave. & 3rd St.)
🏛 Capitol South
𝒞 (202) 544-8088 — **WEB:** www.sonomadc.com
◼ Lunch Sun – Fri   Dinner nightly   **PRICE: $$**

THE SOURCE BY WOLFGANG PUCK ♍⚮

Asian

✗✗ | ♿ 💄 🔥 🍴 🍽   **MAP:** 3-B4

Say what you want—this restaurant is, after all, housed inside the Newseum, a place where free speech is revered—but Wolfgang Puck manages to churn out reliably good food in trademark chic settings, and The Source is certainly no exception to this rule. Step in to find a boisterous first-floor lounge crowned by a second-floor dining room of soft grey banquettes jazzed-up by yellow chairs and glass-walled wine storage.

A new chef has brought a refresh to the menu, which sticks to its flavorsome, pan-Asian vision. A double-cut pork chop rocks garnishes of Massaman curry and grilled pineapple, while jackfruit is the star of a Malaysian-style curry. Then, whole-roasted duck includes sliced breast meat with steamed buns and garlic hoisin as part of the feast.

◼ 575 Pennsylvania Ave. NW (at 6th St.)
🏛 Archives
𝒞 (202) 637-6100 — **WEB:** www.wolfgangpuck.com
◼ Lunch Sat   Dinner Mon – Sat   **PRICE: $$**

THE SOVEREIGN ¶O

Belgian

XX | 🍺 🛋

Tucked down a candlelit alley in Georgetown, The Sovereign takes the dark wood and high tables of the classic bar and warms it up with richly patterned fabrics, red leather chairs, and soft lighting. This place makes no bones about its allegiance to beer, proudly offering over 50 options on draft and more than 300 bottles.

Of course the kitchen celebrates Belgian cuisine as much as it does beer. Items include bitterballen, shrimp croquettes, tartes flambeés, and carbonade flamande—a beer-braised beef stew. It's also easy to see why a street treat like gaufres liégoise are elevated here, thanks to the addition of pistachio paste-flavored whipped cream. But for the real deal, dive into steamed mussels accompanied by deliciously skinny frites.

🔲 1206 Wisconsin Ave. NW (bet. M & Prospect Sts.)
📞 (202) 774-5875 — **WEB:** www.thesovereigndc.com
🔲 Lunch Sat – Sun   Dinner nightly

PRICE: $$

SUSHI OGAWA ¶O

Japanese

XX | 🔲

Sushi Capitol's much-talked-about chef, Minoru Ogawa, now runs the show at this hot spot tucked inside a stunning art deco building in upscale Kalorama Heights. The décor is everything you'd expect from a chic Japanese restaurant: subtly textured walls, honey-hued wood, and minimalist details.

Sushi is front and center here and omakase is certainly the way to go, though an à la carte menu is offered at the handful of tables in the intimate dining room. The fish is from Japan by way of the New Fulton Fish Market in New York City, and some pieces dazzle more than others. Tender baby snapper, torched Japanese barracuda, sea eel paired with octopus and brushed with unagi sauce, and hiramasa with slivered myoga and grated ginger root are among the hits.

🔲 2100 Connecticut Ave. NW (Kalorama Rd. & Wyoming Ave.)
🚇 Dupont Circle
📞 (202) 813-9715 — **WEB:** www.sushiogawa.com
🔲 Dinner Mon – Sat

PRICE: $$$$

SUSHI TARO ✿

Japanese

XX

Sushi aficionados know to give this beloved Dupont Circle gem a pass for its odd location—adjacent to a large-chain pharmacy and accessed by a short flight of steps. However, the interior then opens up into a comfortable and warmly attended dining room. Sushi Taro may offer a solid à la carte and numerous tasting menus, but the overall experience at the omakase counter is truly stellar.

Scoring a meal at said counter proves challenging since seats can only be booked online, via e-mail, 30 days in advance. Once secured, a reservation here grants entrée to a cloistered room where Chefs Nobu Yamazaki and Masaya Kitayama cater to a mere handful of diners.

Following the construct of kaiseki, the meal is a series of artistically composed courses such as grilled marinated tuna cheek or squid ink-tinted soft-shell crab tempura. The meal hits its apex come sushi time when the chefs present a stack of boxes stocked with an immense selection of fish arranged by type, and then invite diners to make selections from this bounty, which are then knifed into sashimi. An equally superb nigiri course follows, allowing further opportunity to delve deeper into the jaw-dropping assemblage.

■ 1503 17th St. NW (bet. Church & P Sts.)
🚇 Dupont Circle
📞 (202) 462-8999 — **WEB:** www.sushitaro.com
■ Lunch Mon – Fri   Dinner Mon – Sat

PRICE: $$$$

TABARD INN

American

MAP: 1-C2

The Tabard Inn has history in the bag; this place is the oldest continuously operating hotel in the city. But before you assume it's just for the blue hair set, take a look at the surprisingly hip crowd who frequent it—and then join them.

Begin with a cocktail in the lounge before heading to the dining room, where the American-focused menu suits the space to a tee. There are a few outliers, like muhammara and house-made hummus, but the selections definitely skew red-white-and-blue: pan-seared duck breast from Maple Leaf Farms in Indiana; sea scallops from Georges Bank; and grilled dry-aged ribeye from Iowa. Artichoke hearts double as bowls for well-seasoned and tasty crabmeat stuffing, and Louisiana gumbo is deconstructed for an unusually artful look.

1739 N St. NW (bet. 17th & 18th Sts.)
Dupont Circle
(202) 331-8528 — **WEB:** www.tabardinn.com
Lunch & dinner daily
PRICE: $$

TABERNA DEL ALABARDERO

Spanish

MAP: 1-B4

When times call for unapologetic, old-world formality, reserve a table at Taberna del Albardero. Regal and resplendent, with everything from the walls and fabrics to the plush carpets awash in vivid red, this is the kind of place where servers donning formal attire deliver white glove service to international dignitaries—the din of a dozen different languages weaving a kind of symphony in the background.

Madrid-native Javier Romero's menu begins with classic Spanish tapas—patatas bravas and gambas al ajillo. Edgier creations may include prawn burgers on ink-tinted buns and arroz cremosa calabaza, a Spanish riff on risotto with tempura-fried Blue Point oysters, butternut squash purée-flavored sauce, and a drizzle of anise liqueur.

1776 I St. NW (entrance on 18th St.)
Farragut North
(202) 429-2200 — **WEB:** www.alabardero.com
Lunch Mon – Fri   Dinner nightly
PRICE: $$$

TAIL UP GOAT ✿

Contemporary

XX | 🍸 &   **MAP:** 2-A3

A trio of veterans from Komi and Little Serow has united to bring D.C. one of its hottest spots. What's with the name? It reflects the Caribbean upbringing of Chef Jon Sybert's wife, Jill Tyler, as well as an island expression to differentiate between goats and sheep: tail up goat, tail down sheep.

This hip bistro welcomes diners with a buzzing bar area where thirst quenchers like the daiquiri of the day or a hibiscus agua fresca call to mind sandy shores. Colorful tiles, light-colored wood furnishings, and pastel accents cement the setting's easy-breezy vibe.

Chef Sybert's menu is a stimulating piece of work that starts off with some serious bread options. The handful of choices are unlike anything previously experienced—take for example the delightfully unorthodox crostini of grilled charred chocolate rye with salt-baked sardines, sweet butter, and pickled beets. Among the pastas, hope to find supple, richly yellow maltagliati dressed with fermented honey sausage, pea shoots, and breadcrumbs. Whole roasted porgy is precisely de-boned and stuffed with ramps, spinach, and capers. Lastly don't miss out on sweets, particularly the crunchy cannolo stuffed with lemon-scented whipped ricotta.

◼ 1827 Adams Mill Rd. NW (bet. Lanier Pl. & Columbia Rd.)
℘ (202) 986-9600 — **WEB:** www.tailupgoat.com
◼ Dinner nightly   **PRICE:** $$

THIP KHAO ☺

Lao

XX | ☂

Having earned herself a loyal following at Bangkok Golden in Falls Church, Chef Seng Luangrath is wowing the crowds in ever-transforming Columbia Heights.

Thip Khao's menu tempts with its sheer variety, from snacks and salads to soups, curries, and a panoply of entrées. Naem khao, a crispy coconut rice salad, bursts with fresh and fragrant flavor, while muu som, cured and slow-cooked pork belly, is wonderfully fatty. The gang deng is delicious, its mildly spicy red chili curry dotted with tender chunks of tofu and crunchy vegetables, but it's the knap paa or Chilean sea bass that really stands out. Brushed with curry paste and coconut cream, then grilled in a banana leaf, you'll find yourself wondering: is it dinner or a present?

■ 3462 14th St. NW (bet. Meridian Pl. & Newton St.)
■ Columbia Heights
℘ (202) 387-5426 — **WEB:** www.thipkao.com
■ Lunch Fri – Sun Dinner nightly

PRICE: $$

TICO ⑂

Latin American

XX | ☞

It may be an offshoot of the Boston original, but Tico stands on its own two feet, thank you very much. Pulsing with energy, it fits right in with this lively U Street neighborhood. The spacious dining room's dark wood furnishings and vibrant murals create the sense of relaxing in a Latin American courtyard—and trust us, once those hibiscus margaritas arrive, the easy-breezy vibe is just beginning.

There is plenty to choose from here, including ceviche (black bass is a good choice); tacos; small plates like black risotto croquettes and lamb meatballs; as well as plancha items like sweet and meaty prawns or sausage (morcilla) and peppers. Tres leches cake, served very cold, closes out the rollicking good time with its silky-sweet perfection.

■ 1926 14th St. NW (bet. T & U Sts.)
■ U St
℘ (202) 319-1400 — **WEB:** www.ticodc.com
■ Lunch Sat – Sun Dinner nightly

PRICE: $$

TOKI UNDERGROUND ⑪○

Japanese

✗

It's easy to miss Toki Underground (it's above The Pug bar). That grungy stretch could be off-putting, and inside, well, it's divey. But it's all good because this just adds to the allure. The room features mostly counter and bar seating in typical ramen style and the décor does nothing to distract diners from the main event: bowls of the steaming stuff.

Toki classic is the signature—a rich yet light broth teeming with thin noodles, pulled pork, soft-poached egg, baby spinach, and a hint of togarashi for just the right amount of razzle-dazzle. Other variations include Taipei curry, kimchi, red miso, and a vegetarian option. There are non-soup offerings as well, like dumplings and tsukemen (dipping) noodles with products sourced from local farms.

■ 1234 H St. NE (bet. 12th & 13th Sts.)
℘ (202) 388-3086 — **WEB:** www.tokiunderground.com
■ Lunch & dinner Mon – Sat   PRICE: ⌘

TOSCA ⑪○

Italian

✗✗✗ | 🎴 ♿ 🖥 🎱

Situated at the base of a nondescript office building, Tosca doesn't initially grab attention. But with modern sophistication and warm, vaguely old-world service, this restaurant caters to an established, moneyed crowd. It's the kind of place where wheeling and dealing over plates of homemade Italian dishes is business as usual.

Pasta is a standout, and while different variations roam Italy for inspiration, almost all share a delicious richness. Scialatielli drenched in a white wine-cream sauce and served with tender rabbit-based ragù has just a hint of sweetness. Then the branzino, though simple, is expertly cooked and seasoned just enough to heighten its fresh flavor. The lengthy wine list is largely Italian, though California is well-represented.

■ 1112 F St. NW (bet. 11th & 12th Sts.)
🅼 Metro Center
℘ (202) 367-1990 — **WEB:** www.toscadc.com
■ Lunch Mon – Fri   Dinner Mon – Sat   PRICE: $$$

2AMYS 😊
Pizza

🍴 | 🍺   **MAP:** 6-A1

Pizza fans can't get enough of this joint and for good reason: three of its wood-fired pies are D.O.C.-certified—meaning they meet the requirements of Italy's VPN (Verace Pizza Napoletana), an association created to protect and promote the Neapolitan pizza. Under its watchful eye, the kitchen must adhere to strict guidelines on everything from ingredients to preparation, ensuring this particular trio of 'za is as classic as it gets. While regulars order from exceptional small plates at the wine bar, there is much on this menu to satisfy non-conformists—like the cockle- and caper-topped vongole or Etna pizza with eggplant confit and olives.

Also check out the wood-fired delights made from house-milled flour at Etto, brought to you by the same dedicated owners.

🔲 3715 Macomb St. NW (bet. 38th St. & Wisconsin Ave.)
📞 (202) 885-5700 — **WEB:** www.2amysdc.com
🔲 Lunch Tue – Sun Dinner nightly   **PRICE: $$**

ZAYTINYA 😊
Mediterranean

🍴🍴 | 🎎 ♿ 🏠 🖥 🛋 🖐   **MAP:** 3-B3

Awash in a palette of cool blue and white with an entire wall artfully decorated with Turkish nazar ornaments (eye-shaped amulets used to ward off evil spirits), Zaytinya speaks to the ease and elegance of the Mediterranean—and indeed this restaurant offers a smorgasbord of Med-influenced flavor. Though large, the dining room is sectioned into cozy nooks, and the warm, friendly service makes it feel especially inviting.

If the look is a little bit of this and a little bit of that, so is powerhouse chef, José Andrés' meze-minded menu. Ouzo-battered catfish skordalia and oyster saganaki are proof that Greek influences run deep, while the wine list is especially far-reaching with bottles from Lebanon and Romania along with surprises from Greece and Turkey.

🔲 701 9th St. NW (at G St.)
🚇 Gallery Pl-Chinatown
📞 (202) 638-0800 — **WEB:** www.zaytinya.com
🔲 Lunch & dinner daily   **PRICE: $$**

MICHELIN IS CONTINUALLY INNOVATING FOR SAFER, CLEANER, MORE ECONOMICAL, MORE CONNECTED AND BETTER ALL AROUND MOBILITY.

Tires wear more quickly on short urban journeys.

TRUE!

You tend to accelerate and brake more often when driving around town so your tires work harder!
If you are stuck in traffic, keep calm and drive slowly.

Tire pressure only affects your car's safety.

FALSE!

Driving with underinflated tires (0.5 below recommended pressure) doesn't just impact handling and fuel consumption, it will take 8,000 km off tire lifespan.
Make sure you check tire pressure about once a month and before you go on vacation or a long journey.

Fitting **2 winter tires** on my car guarantees maximum safety.

FALSE!

In the winter, especially when temperatures drop below 44.5°F, to ensure better road grip, all four tires should be identical and fitted at the same time.

2 WINTER TIRES ONLY =
risk of compromised road grip.

4 WINTER TIRES =
safer handling when cornering, driving downhill and braking.

If you regularly encounter rain, snow or black ice, choose a **MICHELIN Alpin tire**. This range offers you sharp handling plus a comfortable ride to safely face the challenge of winter driving.

MICHELIN
IS COMMITTED

▶ MICHELIN IS THE **GLOBAL LEADER IN FUEL-EFFICIENT TIRES** FOR LIGHT VEHICLES.

▶ **EDUCATING YOUNGSTERS ON ROAD SAFETY FOR BIKES,** NOT FORGETTING TWO-WHEELERS. LOCAL ROAD SAFETY CAMPAIGNS WERE RUN IN **16 COUNTRIES** IN 2015.

QUIZ

1   TIRES ARE BLACK SO WHY IS THE MICHELIN MAN WHITE?

Back in 1898 when the Michelin Man
was first created from a stack of tires,
they were made of natural rubber, cotton
and sulphur and were therefore
light-colored. The composition of tires
did not change until after the First World War
when carbon black was introduced.
But the Michelin Man kept his color!

2   HOW LONG HAS MICHELIN BEEN GUIDING TRAVELERS?

Since 1900. When the MICHELIN guide was published
at the turn of the century, it was claimed that it
would last for a hundred years. It's still around
today and remains a reference with new editions
and online restaurant listings in a number of countries.

3   WHEN WAS THE "BIB GOURMAND" INTRODUCED IN THE MICHELIN GUIDE?

The symbol was created in 1997 but as early as 1954
the MICHELIN guide was recommending "exceptional
good food at moderate prices." Today, it features
on the MICHELIN Restaurants website and app.

If you want to enjoy a fun day out and find out more about Michelin,
why not visit the l'Aventure Michelin museum and shop
in Clermont-Ferrand, France:

www.laventuremichelin.com

MICHELIN
A better way forward

MAPS

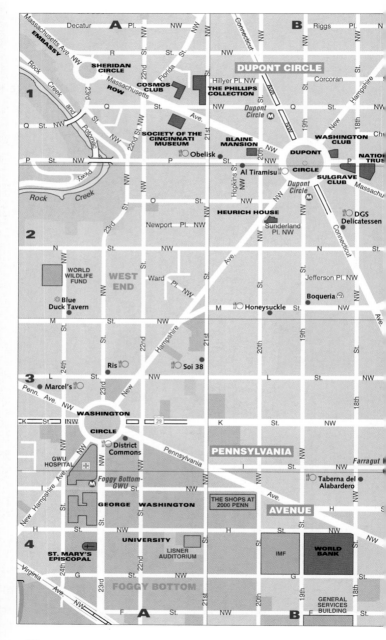

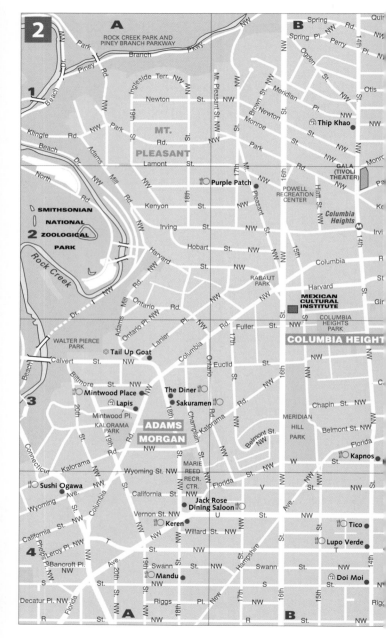

A

B

ROCK CREEK PARK AND
PINEY BRANCH PARKWAY

Spring
Spring Pl. NW
Perry

Quir

14th Pl.

Ogden St.

Otis

1

Park

Beach

Piney
Rd.

Branch
Pkwy.

Ingleside Terr. NW

NW

NW

Mt. Pleasant St. NW

Meridian

Brown St. NW

Newton

Newton
St. NW

NW

Thip Khao

NW

Monroe

NW

Klingle

Rd.

19th St. NW

Park St. NW

Adams Mill Rd. NW

Monroe St. NW

Park

Rd.

NW

GALA
(TIVOLI
THEATER)

Monro

Beach

Dr.

MT.

PLEASANT

16th St. NW

Hiatt St. NW

Pa

Lamont St. NW

Purple Patch

17th St. NW

North Rd.

Kenyon

St.

18th St. NW

POWELL
RECREATION
CENTER

Ke

SMITHSONIAN

NATIONAL

2   ZOOLOGICAL

PARK

Irving St.

NW

NW

*Columbia
Heights*

M

14th

Irvi

15th St. NW

Hobart St.

NW

Columbia

R

Harvard

St.

St. NW

Mill Rd.

Rock Creek

Ontario Rd.

NW

RABAUT
PARK

St. NW

Gir

Adams Mill Rd. NW

Ontario Pl. NW

Lanier Pl. NW

Fuller St.

Harvard St.

MEXICAN
CULTURAL
INSTITUTE

NW

COLUMBIA
HEIGHTS
PARK

Dr.

WALTER PIERCE
PARK

Tail Up Goat

17th St.

Columbia

Rd. NW

Euclid St.

NW

16th St. NW

NW

COLUMBIA HEIGHT

Calvert St. NW

Beach

Biltmore St. NW

20th St. NW

Mintwood Place

Lapis

The Diner

Sakuramen

Ontario Rd.

Champlain St.

NW

NW

Chapin St. NW

NW

C.

3

Mintwood Pl.

19th St. NW

KALORAMA
PARK

**ADAMS
MORGAN**

Kalorama Rd. NW

MERIDIAN
HILL
PARK

Belmont St. NW

Florida

NW

NW

Belmont St. NW

Kapnos

Connecticut

Kalorama

Sushi Ogawa

Columbia Rd. NW

Ave.

Wyoming St. NW

18th St. NW

MARIE
REED
RECR.
CTR.

California St.

Florida

V St. NW

W St. NW

NW

Ave.

NW

St.

4

Wyoming

St. NW

Columbia

Vernon St. NW

Jack Rose
Dining Saloon

U St.

Tico

California St. NW

Keren

Willard St. NW

New Hampshire Ave.

Lupo Verde

NW

T

14th

Phelps Pl. NW

Leroy Pl. NW

20th St. NW

19th St. NW

Swann St. NW

Mandu

Swann St.

NW

Doi Moi

15th St.

N

Bancroft Pl.
NW

Decatur Pl. NW

Florida

18th St. NW

Riggs Pl. NW

17th St.

16th St.

New

S St.

Rigg

R St.

A

NW

B

St. NW

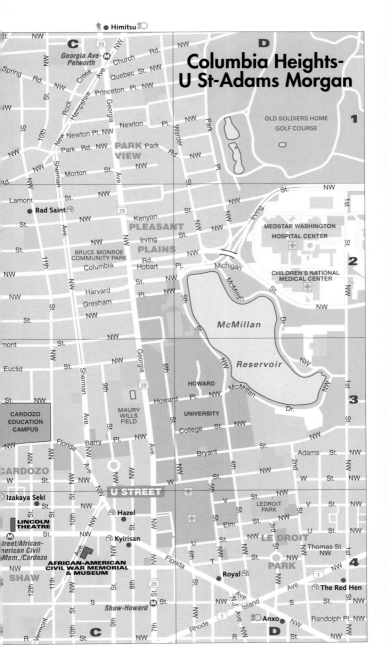

Columbia Heights-
U St-Adams Morgan

Himitsu

Georgia Ave-
Petworth

Spring Rd. NW

Church Rd.

Quebec St. NW

Princeton Pl. NW

Rock Creek

New Hampshire Ave.

Georgia

St.

10th

Newton Pl. NW

Park Rd. NW

Newton Pl.
NW

Sherman

Warder

Park Rd. NW

Park

PARK
VIEW

Morton St. NW

Ave.

NW

St.

D

OLD SOLDIERS HOME
GOLF COURSE

1

Lamont St.

Bad Saint

Kenyon St.

PLEASANT

Ave.

NW

Irving St.

PLAINS

NW

Irving

St.

NW

1st

St. NW

MEDSTAR WASHINGTON
HOSPITAL CENTER

2

11th

BRUCE MONROE
COMMUNITY PARK

Columbia Rd.

Hobart Pl.

NW

Michigan

CHILDREN'S NATIONAL
MEDICAL CENTER

NW

St.

Harvard St.

Gresham Pl.
NW

5th

McMillan

NW

Dr.

St.

mont St.

NW

McMillan

NW

Euclid St.

Sherman

Georgia

6th

NW

McMillan

Reservoir

St. NW

9th

St.

HOWARD

Howard Pl. NW

McMillan

Dr.

NW

1st

3

CARDOZO
EDUCATION
CAMPUS

Ave.

MAURY
WILLS
FIELD

UNIVERSITY

College St.

St.

NW

Florida

Barry Pl. NW

Bryant St.

4th

NW

Adams St. NW

2nd

St. NW

CARDOZO

Ave.

St.

NW

NW

W St.

U STREET

V St.

5th

St.

V St. NW

LEDROIT
PARK

3rd

St. NW

U St. NW

Izakaya Seki

St.

NW

Hazel

Elm St.

LE DROIT

NW

LINCOLN
THEATRE

10th

St. NW

Kyirisan

U St.

Florida

T St.

NW

6th

PARK

Thomas St.
NW

1st

NW

treet/African-
nerican Civil
Mem./Cardozo

AFRICAN-AMERICAN
CIVIL WAR MEMORIAL
& MUSEUM

Ave.

8th

St.

Royal

The Red Hen

NW

11th

St.

12th

SHAW

Vermont

10th

St.

7th

S St.

Shaw-Howard

6th

St.

NW

Rhode

N.J. Ave.

Island

Ave.

Anxo

S St.

Randolph Pl. NW

NW

R St.

R St.

NW

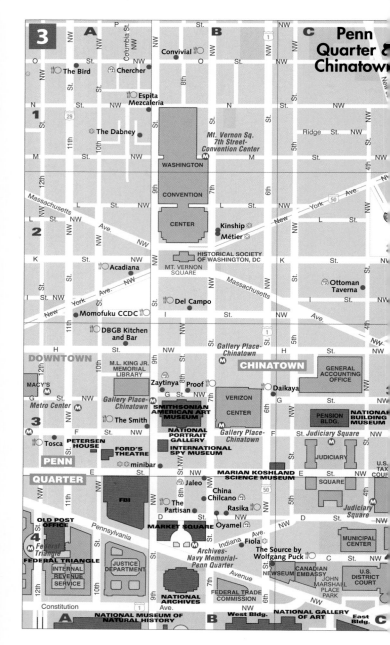

A

B

C

Penn Quarter & Chinatown

P Columbia St. NW

Convivial ↟○

O The Bird ↟○   Chercher ⊕

↟○ Espita Mezcaleria

1

The Dabney ✿

Mt. Vernon Sq. 7th Street-Convention Center

Ridge St. NW

WASHINGTON

CONVENTION

Massachusetts Ave. NW

York Ave. NW

New York 50 Ave.

CENTER

Kinship ✿
Métier ✿

2

↟○ Acadiana

Ottoman ⊕ Taverna

HISTORICAL SOCIETY OF WASHINGTON, DC
MT. VERNON SQUARE

Massachusetts Ave.

↟○ Del Campo

New York Ave.

Momofuku CCDC ●   ↟○

↟○ DBGB Kitchen and Bar

Gallery Place-Chinatown

DOWNTOWN

M.L. KING JR. MEMORIAL LIBRARY

CHINATOWN

GENERAL ACCOUNTING OFFICE

MACY'S

Zaytinya ⊕   Proof ↟○

↟○ Daikaya

Metro Center Ⓜ

Gallery Place-Chinatown Ⓜ

SMITHSONIAN AMERICAN ART MUSEUM

VERIZON CENTER

PENSION BLDG.

NATIONAL BUILDING MUSEUM

Ⓜ **3**

↟○ The Smith

NATIONAL PORTRAIT GALLERY

Gallery Place-Chinatown

Judiciary Square Ⓜ

↟○ Tosca

PETERSEN HOUSE

FORD'S THEATRE

INTERNATIONAL SPY MUSEUM

JUDICIARY

U.S. TAX COU

PENN

✿ minibar ●

MARIAN KOSHLAND SCIENCE MUSEUM

SQUARE

QUARTER

Jaleo ⊕

FBI

↟○ The Partisan

China Chilcano ⊕

Rasika ↟○

Judiciary Square

4 OLD POST OFFICE

Pennsylvania

MARKET SQUARE

Oyamel ⊕

MUNICIPAL CENTER

Ⓜ Federal Triangle

FEDERAL TRIANGLE

JUSTICE DEPARTMENT

Indiana Ave.

Fiola ✿

The Source by Wolfgang Puck ↟○

INTERNAL REVENUE SERVICE

Archives-Navy Memorial-Penn Quarter Ⓜ

Avenue

NEWSEUM

CANADIAN EMBASSY

JOHN MARSHALL PLACE PARK

U.S. DISTRICT COURT

Constitution Ave.

NATIONAL ARCHIVES

FEDERAL TRADE COMMISSION

A NATIONAL MUSEUM OF NATURAL HISTORY

B West Bldg.

NATIONAL GALLERY OF ART

East Bldg. **C**

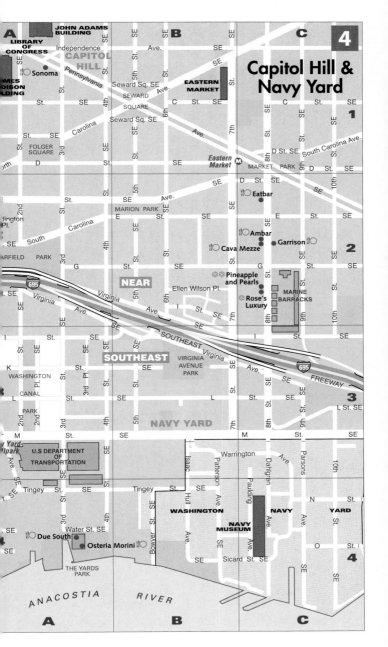

Capitol Hill & Navy Yard

JOHN ADAMS BUILDING

LIBRARY OF CONGRESS

CAPITOL HILL

Independence Ave. SE

MES DISON LDING

Sonoma

Pennsylvania

Seward Sq. SE

SEWARD SQUARE

EASTERN MARKET

Seward Sq. SE

C St. SE

Carolina

FOLGER SQUARE

D St.

Eastern Market

MARKET PARK

D St. SE

South Carolina Ave.

Eatbar

MARION PARK

South Carolina

E St. SE

RFIELD PARK

Ambar

Garrison

Cava Mezze

NEAR

Virginia Ave.

Pineapple and Pearls

Ellen Wilson Pl.

Rose's Luxury

MARINE BARRACKS

SOUTHEAST Virginia

SOUTHEAST

VIRGINIA AVENUE PARK

695 FREEWAY

WASHINGTON PL.

CANAL PARK

NAVY YARD

L St. SE

Yard-
lpark

U.S DEPARTMENT OF TRANSPORTATION

Warrington

Tingey St.

Tingey St.

WASHINGTON NAVY MUSEUM

NAVY YARD

Due South

Water St. SE

Osteria Morini

THE YARDS PARK

Sicard St. SE

ANACOSTIA RIVER

Independence Ave.

4th St.

3rd St.

5th St.

6th St.

7th St.

8th St.

9th St.

10th St.

Isaac

Patterson Ave.

Dahlgren

Parsons

Paulding Ave.

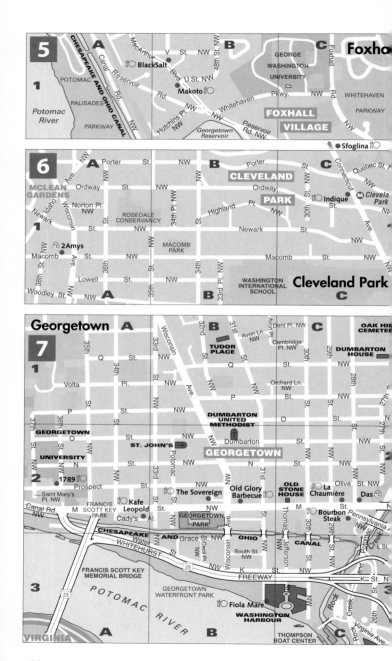

5

CHESAPEAKE AND OHIO Canal

MacArthur Blvd.

V St. NW

A

B

48th St. NW

C

Foxha

BlackSalt

POTOMAC AND

Canal Reservoir Rd.

U St. NW

Makoto

GEORGE WASHINGTON UNIVERSITY

Foxhall Rd.

PALISADES

1

Potomac River

Hutchins Pl. NW

Whitehaven

Pkwy. NW

WHITEHAVEN

PARKWAY

Reservoir Rd. NW

FOXHALL VILLAGE

PARKWAY

Georgetown Reservoir

Sfoglina

6

NW

Porter St.

A

NW

B

Porter St.

C

Quebec St.

Connecticut

MCLEAN GARDENS

Ordway St.

NW

Ordway St.

CLEVELAND

NW

NW

Indique

St.

Cleveland Park

Idaho

Wisconsin

Norton Pl. NW

ROSEDALE CONSERVANCY

34th Pl. NW

Highland Pl. NW

PARK

30th

Ave.

NW

Newark

St.

NW

St.

NW

Newark St.

1

2Amys

Macomb St.

NW

MACOMB PARK

Macomb St.

NW

38th

39th

34th

33rd Pl. NW

Ave.

St.

Lowell St.

NW

NW

WASHINGTON INTERNATIONAL SCHOOL

Cleveland Park

Woodley St.

NW

A

B

C

Georgetown

A

Wisconsin

B

32nd

31st

Avon Pl. NW

Dent Pl. NW

C

OAK HIL CEMETER

7

35th

33rd

St.

NW

St.

TUDOR PLACE

St.

Avon Ln. NW

Cambridge Pl. NW

30th

29th

DUMBARTON HOUSE

1

Q

34th

St.

NW

Ave.

NW

Q

St.

NW

Orchard Ln. NW

St.

NW

28th

Volta

Pl.

NW

P

St.

NW

P

St.

NW

O

St.

NW

St.

NW

St.

NW

27th

37th

36th

GEORGETOWN

O

St.

NW

NW

DUMBARTON UNITED METHODIST

Dumbarton St.

31st

ST. JOHN'S

NW

GEORGETOWN

Potomac

UNIVERSITY

N

St.

NW

N

St.

NW

Olive St. NW

2

1789

Prospect

Saint Mary's Pl. NW

FRANCIS SCOTT KEY PARK

Kafe Leopold

33rd

St.

NW

The Sovereign

Old Glory Barbecue

OLD STONE HOUSE

La Chaumière

Das

Canal Rd. NW

Cady's Al.

GEORGETOWN PARK

Wisconsin Ave.

Thomas

30th

29th

Bourbon Steak

Pennsylvania

CHESAPEAKE

AND

Grace St. NW

Cecil Pl. NW

OHIO

Jefferson

CANAL

Potomac

Rock Creek

K St.

Water

WHITEHURST

South St. NW

28th

FRANCIS SCOTT KEY MEMORIAL BRIDGE

29

FREEWAY

K St. NW

3

POTOMAC

GEORGETOWN WATERFRONT PARK

Fiola Mare

WASHINGTON HARBOUR

Rock Creek

26th

Virginia Ave.

RIVER

VIRGINIA

A

B

THOMPSON BOAT CENTER

C

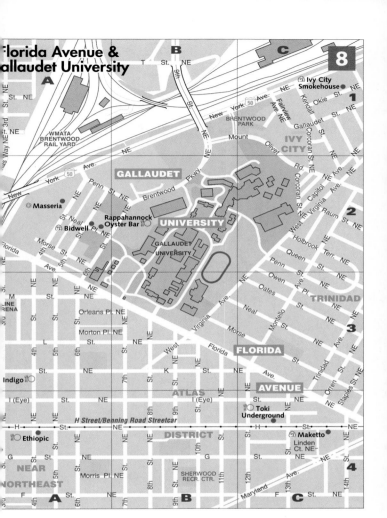

Florida Avenue & Gallaudet University

A B C

1

2

3

4

St. NE

Way NE 3rd
St. NE

WMATA
BRENTWOOD
RAIL YARD

New York 50 Ave.

T St. NE
9th
St.

New York 50 Ave. NE
BRENTWOOD
PARK

Ivy City
Smokehouse

Kendall Okie St. NE
Fairview
Ave. NE
Gallaudet St.
Corcoran St.

Mount
Olive

IVY
CITY

GALLAUDET

Penn St. NE
Brentwood Pkwy.

Masseria

York NE
50
New

Florida

Morse
St. NE
4th
St. Neal
Pl. NE
Bidwell

Rappahannock
Oyster Bar

UNIVERSITY

GALLAUDET
UNIVERSITY

Rd. NE
Corcoran St. NE
West Virginia Ave.
Capitol
Virginia Ave.

Raum St. NE

Holbrook Terr. NE

Queen St. NE

Ave.
5th

6th St. NE

NE
St.
NE
St.
NE

Orleans Pl. NE

Morton Pl. NE
St. NE

West

Virginia Ave.

Morse

Florida

Penn St. NE

Owen Pl. NE
Oates St.

Neal

Montello St.

TRINIDAD

NE

M
LINE
RENA

4th
St.

5th
St.

6th
St.

7th
St.

L St. NE

St. NE

K
St. NE

8th
9th
St. NE

Florida Ave. NE

FLORIDA

AVENUE

Trinidad Ave. NE

Orren St. NE

Staples St. NE

Indigo

I (Eye)

St. NE

NE

7th
St.

8th
St. NE

9th
St.

I (Eye) St. NE

ATLAS

Toki
Underground

H Street/Benning Road Streetcar

H St. NE

DISTRICT

H St. NE

St. NE

Ethiopic

G St. NE

Morris Pl. NE

8th
St.

9th
St. NE

10th
G St. NE

11th
St.

12th
St.

SHERWOOD
RECR. CTR.

13th
St.

Maketto

Linden
Ct. NE

NE

NEAR

NORTHEAST

St.
4th

5th
St.

F St. NE

6th
St.

A

7th
St.

B

9th
St.

Maryland Ave.

F St. NE

C

14th
St.

89

INDEXES

ALPHABETICAL LIST OF RESTAURANTS

A

Acadiana ⑩ 12
Al Tiramisu ⑩ 12
Ambar ⑩ 13
Anxo ⑩ 13

B

Bad Saint ⑭ 14
Bidwell ⑭ 14
Bird (The) ⑩ 15
BlackSalt ⑩ 15
Blue Duck Tavern ✿ 16
Bombay Club ⑩ 17
Boqueria ⑭ 17
Bourbon Steak ⑩ 18

C

Cava Mezze ⑩ 18
Chercher ⑭ 19
China Chilcano ⑭ 19
Convivial ⑩ 20

D

Dabney (The) ✿ 21
Daikaya ⑩ 20
Das ⑭ 22
DBGB Kitchen and Bar ⑩ 22
Decanter ⑩ 23
Del Campo ⑩ 23
DGS Delicatessen ⑩ 24
Diner (The) ⑩ 24
District Commons ⑩ 25
Doi Moi ⑭ 25
Due South ⑩ 26

E

Eatbar ⑩ 26
Espita Mezcaleria ⑩ 27
Estadio ⑩ 27
Ethiopic ⑩ 28

F

Fiola ✿ 29
Fiola Mare ⑩ 28

G

Garrison ⑩ 30
Ghibellina ⑩ 30

H

Hank's Oyster Bar ⑩ 31
Hazel ⑳ 31
Himitsu ⑩ 32
Honeysuckle ⑩ 32

I

Indigo ⑩ 33
Indique ⑩ 33
Inn at Little Washington (The) ✿✿ 34
Iron Gate ⑩ 35
Ivy City Smokehouse ⑳ 35
Izakaya Seki ⑩ 36

J

Jack Rose Dining Saloon ⑩ 36
Jaleo ⑳ 37

K

Kafe Leopold ⑩ 37
Kapnos ⑩ 38
Keren ⑩ 38
Kinship ✿ 39
Komi ✿ 40
Kyirisan ⑳ 41

L

La Chaumière ⊓○ 41
Lapis ⊛ 42
Le Chat Noir ⊓○ 42
Le Diplomate ⊓○ 43
Little Serow ⊓○ 43
Lupo Verde ⊓○ 44

M

Maketto ⊛ 44
Makoto ⊓○ 45
Mandu ⊓○ 45
Marcel's ⊓○ 46
Masseria ⊛ 47
Métier ⊛ 48
Minibar ⊛⊛ 49
Mintwood Place ⊓○ 46
Mirabelle ⊓○ 50
Momofuku CCDC ⊓○ 50

N

Nazca Mochica ⊓○ 51

O

Obelisk ⊓○ 51
Old Glory Barbecue ⊓○ 52
Osteria Morini ⊓○ 52
Ottoman Taverna ⊛ 53
Oval Room (The) ⊓○ 53
Oyamel ⊛ 54

P

Partisan (The) ⊓○ 54
Pearl Dive Oyster Palace ⊛ 55
Pinea ⊓○ 55
Pineapple and Pearls ⊛⊛ 56
Plume ⊛ 57
Proof ⊓○ 58
Purple Patch ⊓○ 58

R

Rappahannock Oyster Bar ⚓   59
Rasika ⚓   59
Red Hen (The) ⚜   60
Ris ⚓   60
Rose's Luxury ✿   61
Royal ⚜   62

S

Sakuramen ⚓   62
1789 ⚓   63
Sfoglina ⚜   63
Smith (The) ⚓   64
Soi 38 ⚓   64
Sonoma ⚓   65
Source by Wolfgang Puck (The) ⚓   65
Sovereign (The) ⚓   66
Sushi Ogawa ⚓   66
Sushi Taro ✿   67

T

Tabard Inn ⚓   68
Taberna del Alabardero ⚓   68
Tail Up Goat ✿   69
Thip Khao ⚜   70
Tico ⚓   70
Toki Underground ⚓   71
Tosca ⚓   71
2Amys ⚜   72

Z

Zaytinya ⚜   72

RESTAURANTS BY CUISINE

AFGHAN

Lapis 🏠   42

AMERICAN

Bidwell 🏠   14
Blue Duck Tavern ❃   16
Dabney (The) ❃   21
Diner (The) 🍴   24
District Commons 🍴   25
Garrison 🍴   30
Honeysuckle 🍴   32
Inn at Little Washington (The) ❃❃   34
Jack Rose Dining Saloon 🍴   36
Mintwood Place 🍴   46
Proof 🍴   58
Red Hen (The) 🏠   60
Ris 🍴   60
1789 🍴   63
Tabard Inn 🍴   68

ASIAN

Doi Moi 🏠   25
Himitsu 🍴   32
Maketto 🏠   44
Momofuku CCDC 🍴   50
Source by Wolfgang Puck (The) 🍴   65

AUSTRIAN

Kafe Leopold 🍴   37

BALKAN

Ambar 🍴   13

BARBECUE

Old Glory Barbecue 🍴   52

BASQUE

Anxo ⓣ⃝ — 13

BELGIAN

Sovereign (The) ⓣ⃝ — 66

CONTEMPORARY

Bird (The) ⓣ⃝ — 15
Kinship ✿ — 39
Métier ✿ — 48
minibar ✿✿ — 49
Oval Room (The) ⓣ⃝ — 53
Pineapple and Pearls ✿✿ — 56
Rose's Luxury ✿ — 61
Sonoma ⓣ⃝ — 65
Tail Up Goat ✿ — 69

DELI

DGS Delicatessen ⓣ⃝ — 24

ETHIOPIAN

Chercher ⊕ — 19
Das ⊕ — 22
Ethiopic ⓣ⃝ — 28
Keren ⓣ⃝ — 38

EUROPEAN

Plume ✿ — 57

FILIPINO

Bad Saint ⊕ — 14
Purple Patch ⓣ⃝ — 58

FRENCH

Convivial ⓣ⃝ — 20
DBGB Kitchen and Bar ⓣ⃝ — 22
La Chaumière ⓣ⃝ — 41
Le Chat Noir ⓣ⃝ — 42
Le Diplomate ⓣ⃝ — 43
Marcel's ⓣ⃝ — 46
Mirabelle ⓣ⃝ — 50

FUSION

Hazel ⊕ — 31
Kyirisan ⊕ — 41

GASTROPUB

Eatbar 🍴 — 26
Partisan (The) 🍴 — 54
Smith (The) 🍴 — 64

GREEK

Cava Mezze 🍴 — 18
Kapnos 🍴 — 38

INDIAN

Bombay Club 🍴 — 17
Indigo 🍴 — 33
Indique 🍴 — 33
Rasika 🍴 — 59

ITALIAN

Al Tiramisu 🍴 — 12
Fiola ❀ — 29
Ghibellina 🍴 — 30
Lupo Verde 🍴 — 44
Masseria ❀ — 47
Obelisk 🍴 — 51
Osteria Morini 🍴 — 52
Sfoglina 🍴 — 63
Tosca 🍴 — 71

JAPANESE

Daikaya 🍴 — 20
Izakaya Seki 🍴 — 36
Makoto 🍴 — 45
Sakuramen 🍴 — 62
Sushi Ogawa 🍴 — 66
Sushi Taro ❀ — 67
Toki Underground 🍴 — 71

KOREAN

Mandu 🍴 — 45

LAO

Thip Khao 🍴 — 70

LATIN AMERICAN

Del Campo 🍴 — 23
Royal 🍴 — 62
Tico 🍴 — 70

MEDITERRANEAN

Decanter ⚫	23
Iron Gate ⚫	35
Komi ✿	40
Pinea ⚫	55
Zaytinya ✿	72

MEXICAN

Espita Mezcaleria ⚫	27
Oyamel ✿	54

PERUVIAN

China Chilcano ✿	19
Nazca Mochica ⚫	51

PIZZA

2Amys ✿	72

SEAFOOD

BlackSalt ⚫	15
Fiola Mare ⚫	28
Hank's Oyster Bar ⚫	31
Ivy City Smokehouse ✿	35
Rappahannock Oyster Bar ⚫	59

SOUTHERN

Acadiana ⚫	12
Due South ⚫	26
Pearl Dive Oyster Palace ✿	55

SPANISH

Boqueria ✿	17
Estadio ⚫	27
Jaleo ✿	37
Taberna del Alabardero ⚫	68

STEAKHOUSE

Bourbon Steak ⚫	18

THAI

Little Serow ⚫	43
Soi 38 ⚫	64

TURKISH

Ottoman Taverna ✿	53

STARRED RESTAURANTS

✿✿

Inn at Little Washington (The)	34
minibar	49
Pineapple and Pearls	56

✿

Blue Duck Tavern	16
Dabney (The)	21
Fiola	29
Kinship	39
Komi	40
Masseria	47
Métier	48
Plume	57
Rose's Luxury	61
Sushi Taro	67
Tail Up Goat	69

BIB GOURMAND

Bad Saint	14
Bidwell	14
Boqueria	17
Chercher	19
China Chilcano	19
Das	22
Doi Moi	25
Hazel	31
Ivy City Smokehouse	35
Jaleo	37
Kyirisan	41
Lapis	42
Maketto	44
Ottoman Taverna	53
Oyamel	54
Pearl Dive Oyster Palace	55
Red Hen (The)	60
Royal	62
Sfoglina	63
Thip Khao	70
2Amys	72
Zaytinya	72

UNDER $25

Chercher ☺   19
Daikaya ◖○   20
Diner (The) ◖○   24
Indigo ◖○   33
Keren ◖○   38
Purple Patch ◖○   58
Sakuramen ◖○   62
Toki Underground ◖○   71

Tell us what you think about our products.

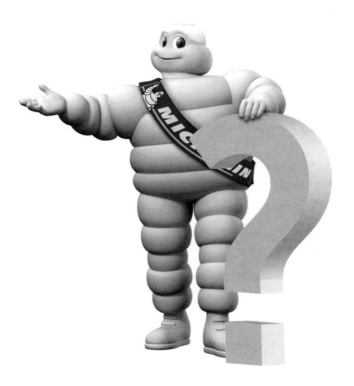

Give us your opinion

satisfaction.michelin.com

MICHELIN TRAVEL PARTNER

Société par actions simplifiées au capital de 11 288 880 EUR
27 Cours de l'Ile Seguin - 92100 Boulogne Billancourt (France)
R.C.S. Nanterre 433 677 721

© 2017 Michelin Travel Partner – All right reserved
Dépôt légal septembre 2017
Printed in Canada - septembre 2017
Printed on paper from sustainably managed forests

Impression et Finition : Transcontinental (Canada)